Theologies and Liberation
in Peru

Theologies and Liberation in Peru

The Role of Ideas in Social Movements

Milagros Peña

Temple University Press
Philadelphia

Temple University Press, Philadelphia 19122
Copyright © 1995 by Temple University. All rights reserved
Published 1995
Printed in the United States of America

⊗ The paper used in this book meets the requirements of the American
National Standard for Information Sciences—Permanence of Paper for
Printed Library Materials, ANSI Z39.48-1984

Text design by Ellen C. Dawson

Library of Congress Cataloging-in-Publication Data
Peña, Milagros, 1955–
    Theologies and liberation in Peru : the role of ideas in social
movements / Milagros Peña.
        p. cm.
    Includes bibliographical references and index.
    ISBN 1-56639-294-2 (alk. paper)
    1. Catholic Church—Peru—History—20th century.
2. Christianity and politics—Catholic Church—History—20th
century. 3. Liberation theology—History. 4. Peru—Church
history—20th century 5. Peru—
History—1968– I. Title.
    BX1484.2.P46 1995
    282'.85'09045—dc20   94-36758

To the memory of my mother,
Milagros Amparo Martínez López
(June 20, 1937–May 1, 1993)

CONTENTS

Preface

The strategies of protesters (strikers, land squatters, and worker groups) have led some Catholic officials in Latin America to publicize their opposition to political activism and others to support it. I argue that the retrenchment policies whereby the Catholic Church in Peru and elsewhere opposed liberation theology and its proponents in the 1980s were linked to a general opposition to decentralizing power within the Church and to popular political protests. More important, the Catholic right in Peru, under the direction of the Sodalitium Vitae movement and others, succeeded in mobilizing institutional resources against liberation theology and developing a theology of reconciliation as an alternative to liberation theology.

Preparation for this book involved the collection and analysis of several bodies of evidence. Using oral histories methodology, I interviewed key figures behind the liberation theology, Sodalitium Vitae, and Opus Dei movements in Peru; bishops and priests representing the different camps; Church activists; and other laypeople on both sides. The Opus Dei movement is discussed only as part of the Catholic right's mobilization against liberation theology, which facilitated coalition formations with the Sodalitium Vitae movement. Because so much of each group's ability to mobilize support depended on the backing of high-ranking officials, I interviewed central figures of the Peruvian Episcopate, as well as two former government officials. A complete list of persons interviewed is found in the Appendix.

Books, newspapers, and archival documents allowed for comparisons and validation of the interviews. My material was gathered principally in Peru, many primary and secondary sources from the archives of the Bartolomé de Las Casas Institute (Rimac, Lima), La Pontificia Universidad Catolica de Lima, La Universidad de Piura, and the Christian feminist organization Talitha Cumi.

Translations from the interviews and other Spanish-language sources are mine. Thus, interpretation and analysis of these materials are my sole responsibility.

It is often said that no book is the effort of any single individual. This book is no exception. It is a testimony to those who gave their lives to the civil rights movement. My uncle Federico Lora participated in that struggle, more precisely, in the Latino struggle, challenging me to think critically and to pursue the same dreams, which shaped my interest in this project.

The book was supported by a State University of New York at Stony Brook Fellowship and by a Bowling Green (Ohio) State University Faculty Research Grant. The Departments of Ethnic Studies and Sociology at Bowling Green facilitated the research by providing departmental resources and course reductions from teaching.

I thank the people of Peru and the foreign missionaries working in Peru who opened their homes, shared their stories, and provided crucial material for this book but whose identities must remain anonymous for obvious reasons. Openly, I would like to thank the Catholic University of Lima (La Pontificia Universidad Catolica de Lima) for allowing me to use its libraries and archives and for writing letters to other institutions that helped further my research. The Bartolomé de Las Casas Institute was invaluable to me; the staff there spent many hours helping me gather historical materials. Talitha Cumi, a feminist organization based in Lima, provided access to other archival material about the Catholic Church in Peru. The University of Piura also provided help in gathering historical data.

I am indebted to Lewis Coser, Michael Schwartz, Richard Williams, and Michael Zweig for their critiques in the initial stages of my writing. I thank Michael Schwartz for the many hours we debated and for his moral support. Wanda Olivera, during my first stay in Peru, took care of many of my day-to-day affairs. Ken Sperber and Sara Collas paid my bills and looked after my car. So many friends—Lorraine Ali, Lillian Ashcraft-Eason, Gene Argentina, Betty Bolden, Alice Calderonello, Patty Daye, María Freitas, Ann-Marie Lancaster, Patrick McGuire, Peggy O'Neill, Linda Pertusati, Jon Spencer, Lynn Vianni, and Opportune Zongo, to name only a few—in one way or another helped to make this book a reality. Bonnie Fink, Doris Braendel, the editorial staff at Temple University Press, and anonymous reviewers provided insightful comments during the revision stages.

Two people to whom I am forever indebted for their support throughout this project are my husband, Fred Hamann, and my sister, Jane Nuñez. My mother passed away unexpectedly as I was working on the manuscript, and without Fred and Jane I would have found it difficult to continue. This book is a testimony to the memory of both my mother, Milagros Amparo Martínez López, and my father, Obtacilio Peña Tejada, because in many ways it is a book about poor people's struggles and their sacrifices to make life better for their children.

Theologies and Liberation
in Peru

CHAPTER ONE

Liberation and Reconciliation

Clashing Political Interests

When liberation theology made its debut in Latin America in the early 1970s, it opened a new chapter in Catholic Church history. From Central America to South America, clamors for solidarity with the poor were heard from within the Latin American Church. Even bishops such as Oscar Romero of El Salvador, a product of that country's status quo, eventually joined the protest—and was assassinated as a result. The response to poor people's movements by Catholic progressives throughout Latin America during this period and beyond has been remarkable.

Liberation theology has its opponents, however, and the conservative attack has gone beyond a war of words. Priests, sisters, and laypeople—pressured by the Vatican and by conservative bishops—have lost jobs; some have been driven from the Church. And yet despite the attacks, liberation theology continues to have appeal. For many, it represents the view that "true commitment to people, involving the transformation of the reality by which they are oppressed, requires a theory of transforming action" (Freire 1970, 120). That is, they see liberation theology as providing a moral ethic requiring not only love for one's neighbor but action on behalf of that neighbor. In line with that thinking, Latin American Catholics and Protestants have come to view the liberationist ethic as one that involves partnership with and commitment to poor people's movements. They recognize that transforming society means transforming a way of life that privileges some and marginalizes others. Coming to that recognition has been part of a long historical process in Latin America. Some say that this attitude may have been driven in part by the success of the Cuban Revolution in 1959, which had a tremendous impact on the psyche of many Latin Americans (Gotay 1981; Pásara 1986; Vidales 1993). Cuba became for the Latin American left the symbol of victory over the political and economic hegemony of the United States and of Latin America's own privileged classes. In many ways the Cuban Revolution unleashed the attempt to defeat a social order that had been established with the arrival of the Spanish conquistador and that had gone more or less undisturbed until 1959 (Pásara 1986, 15). More importantly, the Cuban Revolution showed poor people's movements that it was possible to have a revolution and to win against enormous odds. Moreover, the triumph in Cuba in 1959 went beyond touching the lives of third world revolutionaries; it touched sectors of unlikely allies—namely, members of the Catholic hierarchy.

But other historical factors also came into play in the emergence of liberation theology. Proponents were influenced by an activism that arose from their involvement in the Catholic Action movement, which preceded the Cuban Revolution by at least two decades and liberation theology by at least three. Catholic Action in Latin America started as a workers' movement in the 1930s and 1940s and in a sense was a precursor to liberation theology. It nurtured many individuals who later became involved in liberation theology—among them, its noted Peruvian spokesman Father Gustavo Gutiérrez and three of his closest friends in Peru: Bishop José Dammert Bellido, an advocate of liberation theology and a strong supporter of Gutiérrez; and the Alvarez Calderón brothers, Jorge and Carlos, members of one of the Lima's elite families. Other supporters came through the ranks of the Catholic Action youth movement, La Unión Nacional de Estudiantes Catolicos (UNEC), or the National Union of Catholic Students. These individuals became transformed not only by such political events as the Cuban Revolution but by other revolutionary movements that would characterize Latin America in the decade that followed.

The political climate of the 1960s pushed theological thought and writing beyond the scope of Catholic Action. In the words of Father Gutiérrez, "Everywhere people were coming to the realization that the class struggle had become part of Latin America's economic, social, political, cultural, and religious reality" (1973, 273). For Latin America's Catholics and Protestants alike, solidarity with poor people's movements came to mean a whole new way of talking about Christian ethics and class struggles. In the sociohistorical milieu of the 1960s and 1970s, "liberation theology brought a conscience to Christians concerning the problems of the poor, and it has shown that it is not possible to speak about God without talking about the poor" (Gutiérrez 1988a).

Liberation theology influenced not only the larger picture but the conscience of individuals. That is, it transformed people into advocates of social justice, forcing them to see that their Christianity could not be genuine without it. For many, the message behind liberation theology also implied that the Catholic Church itself had to be transformed, from a voice for the status quo to a voice for the marginalized. Thus, where the

Brazilian educator Paulo Freire and others gave church people, social workers, and organizers a new approach to working with poor people, liberation theologians provided religious language that heralded a new brand of Christianity.

The struggle for liberation in Latin America took Catholic activism to new heights, producing changes in the political sphere, putting Church resources at the disposal of protesters, and producing a new breed of politicized Church activists. Many activists came to see that poor people were determined to bring about social change through political action, with or without the approval of their institutional churches. Thus, when political skirmishes arose between protesters and local governments, priests, sisters, and Catholic layworkers found themselves having to choose whether or not to side with the protesters. Many did: in Father Gutiérrez's words, "What evolved was a clear option in favor of the oppressed and their liberation" (1973, 102).

This new posture also meant reevaluating the life-styles of the clergy, calling into question the meaning of the structure and function of the priesthood and the Catholic Church itself. For that reason, the history of the emergence of liberation theology warns students of religion that not all aspects of religious activity are conservative and favor the status quo. Religion is not necessarily a functional, reproductive, or conservative force in society; it may instead be a major (or even the only) channel for bringing about social revolution (Maduro 1977, 366). This view has shaped the writing of this book.

Many of the students, teachers, Catholic priests and sisters, and Church activists who embraced liberation theology during the 1960s were products of prestigious Catholic education, but, like the liberation theologians, they became radicalized by contemporary events. Many of these same people are now at the heart of political dissent in Latin America and have used their intellectual skills in the service of various protest movements. Versed in philosophy, the social sciences, education, and other fields, they have been able to apply that knowledge to the advancement of the political agenda of poor people's movements.

Father Gutiérrez, for example, as a seminarian, completed graduate studies at Catholic institutions in Louvain, Belgium, and Lyon, France, where he distinguished himself in theology. In these schools he was exposed to world-class scholars in theology, philosophy, and the social sciences. And because other students from Latin America tended to congregate in the same schools, he became part of a community of intellectuals who were stimulated by the emerging theology of liberation.

Many of the scholars whom Gutiérrez met at Louvain went on to develop their own versions of liberation theology in their respective countries. Among them were Luis Segundo of Uruguay, the Chilean sociologist Renato Poblete, Camilo Torres of Colombia, François Hurtard of Belgium, and Argentinean philosophy professor Rafael Brown (Gutiérrez 1988a). Father Jorge Alvarez Calderón, a cornerstone of the Catholic Action worker movement in Peru, was also in the group. The point of this history is simple: though some may believe that these individuals have been slow to achieve a sense of their own national identity, it is nevertheless true that the Church's marked influence over their education did not deter them from becoming voices of protest. I argue that in large measure it was exposure to the Catholic Action movement that served to awaken initially in people like these an instinct for social justice. In other words, to the Church's appeal during the Great Depression on behalf of workers, and its making their problems under capitalism a major concern for Christians, became part of the Catholic Action generation's conscience. Serving in Catholic Action organizations only strengthened relations with poor people's movements. And that was why the Catholic Action phase in the experience of many Catholic activists was so important: it provided opportunities for the then blossoming liberationists to meet one another and to form organizational networks that would facilitate the dissemination of liberation theology and support for its principles.

One must remember, however, that without the social crises that came to a head in the 1960s in Latin America, liberation theology would not have had such significant meaning there. Latin America's liberation theologians became important to a host of poor people's movements because they took their positions as privileged members of an institutional elite (the Catholic Church) and their intellectual skills (which allowed them to manipulate religious language) and put them at the service of these movements. This cadre of intellectuals became immersed in the language and culture of protest groups and came to frame their theological language in political/religious/cultural terms. As the intellectual participants of a profound social movement, they became an integral part of the collective life of poor people's struggles, advocates of reform and sometimes even of revolution. But critical to this process was a historical moment in which these theologians found themselves struggling to align their religious world views with the social reality that was shaping people's lives around them. And that critical historical moment for the Latin American liberation theologians occurred during the 1960s and 1970s.

At that time in Peru, for example, an economic crisis was coming to a head. The crisis increased insurgency activity, which in turn increased military activity, and all these forces put increasing pressure on urban centers as peasants flocked to the cities to find refuge from violence and poverty. Focusing on Peru as a case study will allow the reader to see the intricate network of relationships that gave historical meaning to liberation theology, how it transformed people's lives and defined a country's history for over two decades—and finally, how its opponents mobilized in an effort to eliminate it. Thus, we will examine the emergence of liberation theology in Peru not only in an effort to understand how a group of intellectuals trained primarily for the priesthood came to be advocates of social change but also in order to analyze the consolidation of opposition.

Liberation theology was birthed at a time when many Catholics and Protestants who were pushing for support for poor people's movements were trying to make their social justice messages more meaningful to a politicized constituency and to put their churches' institutional resources at the disposal of their causes. In that context, liberation theology became the vehicle for garnering support of poor people's causes. In Peru the social location of the theologians as high-status members of an elite institution, the Catholic Church, allowed them to use institutional resources more efficiently.

In Latin America, and Peru specifically, liberation theology is an idea that has been at the forefront of support for poor people's causes. Its status as part of the multifaceted response to the socioeconomic inequities that exist in Latin America bears directly on our discussion of the interplay between ideas and how social actors make them useful to social movements. As sociologist Max Weber once said, ideas have "like switchmen determined the tracks along which action has been pushed by the dynamic of interest" (1946, 280). The challenge is to analyze geopolitical circumstances by coming to understand that not just ideas but material and ideational interests together govern human conduct. The individuals who profess liberation theology must be studied in historical context. Why and how they have presented their theological language to its intended audience must be seen in the context of a social movement, and social movements must be understood "in the material and ideological context of the societies in which they emerge" (Ferree and Miller 1985, 43).

Like the theology of liberation, the theology of reconciliation emerged at a time of great economic and political instability, but different sets of motivating circumstances shaped the two ideological constructs. The emergence of the theology of reconciliation and its subsequent alliance with proponents of Opus Dei (a conservative Catholic organization of Spanish origin) can be attributed to ideological dissonance with liberationists over the latter's dismantling of long-established religious and economic icons and, particularly, over the infiltration of Marxist analysis into the religious sphere. Followers of the Sodalitium Vitae movement, which opposes liberation theology, articulated the theology of reconciliation by using the popular aspects of liberationism to call for a return to traditionalism and to official Catholic teachings, which, they say, reject the bulk of liberation theology. Yet although Sodalitium Vitae undoubtedly reflects a sincere commitment to a set of ideals, its adherents' attack on liberation theology is also motivated by political disagreement with the interests and strategies of the popular sector.

This book attempts to show how theologies and theologians as intellectuals came to play important roles in articulating ideas particularly useful to popular movements, on the one hand, and, on the other hand, to those opposing popular movements. To have a dialectical understanding of the role the Catholic Church plays in Latin America, particularly in Peru, is to see that the rise, fall, and resurgence of revolutionary ideas in Christian thought are intimately tied to the sociohistorical reality of the moment. Therefore, to make sense of the conflict within the Latin American Catholic Church over liberation theology is to understand social change by looking at the dialectical interests of particular groups. Seeing the conflict over liberation theology is seeing a particular people's religious conflict as it relates both to class struggle and to their search for national identity. The popular movements in Peru have been "Peru's historical process toward an emancipation and democratization of the oppressed" (Kudó 1982, 120). If this statement is accurate, then that historical process has brought its struggles to all levels of Peru's institutions, including the Church.

One note of caution should be made here: whatever the advances achieved by liberation theology, even this progressive movement has been criticized for its silence on women's issues. This accusation was repeated in my interviews with members of women's groups who found it difficult to run community projects where local bishops or priests—no matter how "progressive" otherwise—disagreed with them over their activities. Sometimes confrontations arose between a women's group and a local bishop or priest about funding women's programs. For many women's groups, one fact has not changed: whether the Church hierarchy is conservative or progressive, power remains in the hands of a male-dominated power structure.

This area of study is very extensive and for that reason is not the subject of discussion here. The significance of this book lies instead in its consideration of social protest as a significant element in the repertoire of religiously motivated action. Specifically, it tries to understand the process by which ideology is transformed into theology and adapted to a new set of social circumstances, and to that end it analyzes the impact that liberation theology has had in Latin America as a motivating ideology among religious people who have identified themselves with popular protest. It also analyzes the social circumstances under which countermovements emerge within the same institutional frame.

More generally, the book is concerned with the impact of religious institutions on social change, the influence of ideologies on the outcome of social movements, and the effect of the social location of certain individuals on the mobilization process of a movement. It is important to analyze the circumstances in which intellectuals in social movements become the source of the ideologies that guide and even create social action. No one can deny that some groups within the Catholic Church, influenced by liberation theology, have sustained a movement that has influenced Latin America politics— sometimes profoundly—and thus demonstrated the viability of organized religion as an institutional vehicle of protest. This example also highlights the important role that ideology can play in generating or maintaining social protest. By investigating the process by which liberation theology in Peru appealed to already politically mobilized religious groups, we can better understand the conditions and actions that create religious dissent and the role that religious ideology can play during moments of political unrest.

Many sociologists, primarily resource mobilization theorists, argue that the extent of a group's protest depends upon the extent of the resources under that group's collective control. It cannot be assumed however, that *material* resources are the only ingredients of successful mobilization; ideology and theory are also necessary, as liberation theology's usefulness to insurgencies and protest movements demonstrates. Indeed, the study of liberation theology in Peru fits neatly into recent models of organized protest that stress the importance of communications networks, broad-based constituencies, and effective preexisting leadership. It allows students of religion and social movements to pursue a number of questions. How do intellectuals come to resonate with movement goals and strategies? How do they use their intellectual skills to provide an ideological ethic that bridges more than one protest population? And how do ideas affect the course of social actions? One way to tackle those questions is to look at "the linkage of individual and social movement organization interpretive interests, values, and beliefs and social movement activities, goals, and ideology as congruent and complimentary"; in other words, if framed correctly, ideas can "function to organize experience and guide action, whether individual or collective" (Snow et al. 1986, 464).

Theologians in Peru bridged constituencies and networks by providing an ideological framework compatible with ideologically overlapping constituencies. Recognizing this phenomenon is crucial to understanding the relationship between the theologian and his or her protest community. Because of the central and visible role played by liberation theology in arousing polarities of resistance within a conservative Church, it is an ideal focus for considering these issues.

Religious leaders, both as subjects and as leaders of protest movements, can be dynamic social forces of change. Because they have access to the core of their religious organization's resources, they exercise extensive influence. Their power base also often includes the availability and potential recruitment of powerful Church leaders. Thus, as members of the very same communities that protesters live in, Church leaders are affected by and must respond to the local crises of their communities, whether they side with or oppose protesters. Sometimes unexpected support from these individuals provides new outcomes and success for protest populations. In Latin America, the response of some bishops to labor and land struggles produced positive results for protesters, showing that the access to religious power can be a source of social power, whether for change or for stability (McGuire 1981, 202).

The transformation of the religious individuals who guided the two movements discussed here was not trivial: the social contradictions of their own religious meanings made them face inconsistencies in their life-styles. Roman Catholic clergy in Latin America have been able to challenge the politico-economic powers of their countries because they form part of an organization with an international base. If their religious organization had had only a local base of power and authority, the clergy would more likely have been suppressed or co-opted by established national politico-economic powers (Westhues 1973). It was their connectedness to this source of power—which at the time was itself undergoing a liberalization process—to which Latin American liberation theologians owe their success and influence.

With liberation theology, the skills of an intellectual elite coupled with the wisdom of an articulate popular constituency created dramatic social changes. Liberation theology swept through Peru and the rest of Latin America because events in the period were demanding dramatic changes in the religious as well as the political sphere. Together, these forces proposed and sponsored a vision of institutional change that included the development of a powerful network at national and international levels, the mobilization of religious popular constituencies, the recruitment of traditional intellectuals, the recruitment of influential Church and political figures, and the creation of a set of ideas attractive to both a religiously and a politically charged population.

These factors came together not only to create a successful religious movement but to generate a network capable of sustaining itself even when faced later with the threat of institutional censure. The emergence of this phenomenon is a credit to the popular movements of Peru, which served to awaken in traditional intellectuals a sense of commitment—not necessarily because some of these intellectuals came from popular sectors but because their religious convictions were shown to be inconsistent with their life-styles. Liberation theology bridged the world of the "traditional" and the "organic" intellectual. Unlike traditional intellectuals, who are academically trained, organic intellectuals have been trained by their life experiences and bring new insights to the articulation of social problems. It has long been believed that "every social group, coming into existence on the original terrain of an essential function in the world of economic production, creates together with itself, organically, one or more strata of intellectuals which give it homogeneity and an awareness of its own function not only in the economic but also in the social and political fields" (Gramsci 1987, 5). Here, organic intellectuals—represented by Church activists and others not formally trained in theology or the social sciences—engaged Father Gustavo Gutiérrez and his circle of traditional intellectuals in exchanges about the meaning of Christian living. Therefore, it can be argued that some religious figures not only produced the ideological underpinnings of a radical religious movement but were themselves sustained by the networks and environments connected with that movement.

This book suggests that the religious intellectual is a church leader who articulates, in religious language, the symbolic meaning of the intellectual life of the region's social movements. In the Latin American context, the adaptive process of ideas in a movement's life was central in some instances to making linkages with the popular sector and in other instances to opposing those linkages. The challenge of popular protest combined with an articulated religious-social consciousness provided both political and religious meaning, but when that meaning challenged established beliefs, others used a different theological language to refute it. Because people tend to act on the basis of some meaning system, the definition of issues, actors, and events often becomes a matter of constant contention (Gamson 1988, 219).

Followers of the Sodalitium Vitae movement contend that liberation theology, because of its ties to the left, is misguided Catholicism; in their attack on liberation theology they have succeeded in pushing forward a theology of reconciliation. Sodalitium Vitae followers look to replace liberation theology, arguing that the meaning system they appeal to is a more legitimate course of Catholic social teaching. The scores of conservatives dissatisfied with the liberationist program regrouped in the late 1970s, mobilized their opposition, and began to stage successive attacks on liberation theology. But even early on in their attacks those conservative factions had to recognize that the Church had been forced to take poor people's movements seriously. Thus, it was not enough for reconciliationists simply to offer traditional interpretations of Catholic teachings; that thinking had been successfully challenged in the 1960s and 1970s. So, to the credit of liberation theology, reconciliationists have included references to the poor in their theological language.

Whatever liberation theology is, it made a contribution to an already existing insurgency that was sparked and exists outside the jurisdiction of the Church. This book identifies ways in which theologians have had something to offer under circumstances in which traditionally they would have had nothing to offer. Confronted by their own life contradictions, some religious leaders can and do assume very radical positions, even when they face the threat of censure or expulsion from the Church. That is how many Catholic priests, sisters, and laypeople have come to see their mission with liberation theology.

In Peru and elsewhere, theologians not only commited to poor people's movements but became the articulators and transmitters of a theological model that calls for activism in concert with the poor. This articulation process could not have developed as it did without such individuals, who partook of and became involved in poor people's struggles. Many liberation theologians used their influence to support these causes; similarly, Opus Dei and Sodalitium Vitae used their influence to reject what they saw as politicized Church teachings. What is important to analyze is the sociohistorical context in which the two sides came to compete in Peru's political arena.

The mobilization of conservative bishops in Peru has depended on the success of the theology of reconciliation to garner the support of a broadly based constituency, much as liberation theology has done. This kind of ideological connection is possible because "each struggle often takes place in a particular issue arena"; that is why, "for every challenge, there is a relevant discourse—a particular set of ideas and symbols that are used in the process of constructing meanings relevant to the struggle," and "to achieve and sustain mobilization, a challenger must participate in such discourse" (Gamson 1988, 221). The coalitions that formed came to depend on how well an articulate intellectual base was able to legitimate its actions among other floating populations of sympathizers.

The Issues

A basic understanding of the social movement processes by which liberation theology emerged is necessary equipment for assessing and understanding the social conditions under which new ideology may arise either to guide mass protest or to thwart it. Critical to this analysis is an understanding of the history that placed the Roman Catholic Church in sole control over the educational and cultural institutions of Peru. After discussing the impact of anticlericalism on the political movements of the 1920s and the emergence of Catholic Action movements in Peru in the 1930s and 1940s, this book goes on to show the significance of the historical transformation that the Latin American Catholic Church underwent just prior to the emergence of liberation theology. This earlier history helps to clarify how the radicalization that characterized the Catholic Church in the 1950s and 1960s produced the generation of radicals who have come to be known as liberation theologians. Historical data are important for placing the individuals who emerged as liberationists within the general changes that were transforming the Catholic Church in those two decades and in showing how influential liberation theology became in promoting poor people's movements and in what ways liberation theologians advanced their causes.

Only by examining the historical context in which people such as Father Gustavo Gutiérrez emerged to become proponents of liberation theology can we understand how liberationism became prominent in Peru. We need to observe the relevant parts of the lives of the people at the center of liberation theology, including the circle of friendships and the access to organizational networks that have been at their disposal. And, because social movements can fizzle or lose strength for a number of reasons, we also need to examine why liberation theology came under attack. The climate of excitement over liberation theology changed dramatically in the 1980s, and with the support of a conservative pope in the Vatican, the Catholic right in Peru and elsewhere began to attack liberation theology. Subsequently, adherents of the Latin American Catholic right were able to take advantage of the fact that in the 1980s people were growing weary of guerrilla warfare and to promote the notion that liberation theology was associated with Marxist ideology, allowing them to lead a fairly successful campaign against it.

In Peru (as the case study), given the violence fueled by confrontations between popular protesters and the government in the late 1970s and by the emergence of the Maoist-Leninist guerrilla group Sendero Luminoso (Shining Path), the Catholic right began accusing liberationists of promoting an ideology that supported violence. Using that association, conservative Catholic bishops organized and mobilized themselves to expel from their parishes sisters and priests whom they deemed adherents of liberation theology or Marxists. This tactic has served to help the Catholic right reorganize its parishes, reclaim control over the theological teachings of churchgoers, and redirect Church resources in support of their fight against liberation theology.

That mobilization raises important questions for students of social movements. If liberation theology was so successful in the 1960s and 1970s in mobilizing sympathy for poor people's movements, what historical circumstances changed in the 1980s and 1990s that allowed countermovements to stage successful attacks on liberation theology? This book explores some historical factors that help explain why the tide shifted. It also explores the impact of intellectuals and ideology on social movement mobilization processes in a religious context.

Spreading the Word

Liberation theology was, in a sense, formally introduced to the world in 1968, at the second meeting of the Latin American Bishops' Council (Consejo Episcopal Latinoamericano, or CELAM) in Medellín, Colombia. There, Father Gustavo Gutiérrez and several other theologians emerged as leading advocates of Church reform, calling for social and economic justice for Latin America's poor. At that same 1968 meeting, bishops and priests produced the first position document that made what came to be called "a preferential option for the poor." Advocates of this stance assumed that attacking social and economic inequities meant attacking the institutions that produce them. From Medellín on, liberation theology has meant solidarity and concern for the poor as a fundamental religious and ethical concern quite different from any other position the Church had taken in the past.

For proponents of this new position, the liberation process demanded "participation both in the transformation of social structures and in effective political action" (Gutiérrez 1973, 46). In other words, in the struggle for the liberation of the oppressed in society, people were expected to go out to search for new ways to narrow the enormous gap between the rich and poor in Latin America and throughout the third world. This search is what is involved in the term "politicization." To be politicized means to have increasing awareness, in breadth and depth, of the many complexities that a process toward fundamental social change requires (Gutiérrez 1973).

This position marked a major shift from the policies set earlier by the Catholic Church. Two papal encyclicals that have been used to establish official Catholic teaching—Leo XIII's "Rerum Novarum," published in 1891, and Pius XI's "Quadragesimo Anno," published in 1931—affirmed concern for the plight of workers and the inherent problem of labor exploitation in capitalism. But both encyclicals were firm in their rejection of Marxism or *any* socialist alternatives to capitalism. Indeed, since 1891 the Vatican's social teaching has tended to reject political concepts of socialism: only during the tenure of Popes John XXIII and Paul VI (1958–78) did the attitude toward socialism change for a while. Paul VI, for example, acknowledged that the Church would only be enriched by open debates with socialists, and this new openness allowed liberal-to-leftist priests within the Catholic Church to pursue exchanges with socialists and to sympathize with the leftist ideologies the popular sectors were adopting in their protest movements.

One dimension of the definition of the popular sector in Latin America is that it directs attention to the ideas, beliefs, practices, and conditions of poor people, however defined, and to the kinds of ties that bind them to institutions of power, privilege, and meaning (Levine 1986, 6). Consequently, for the more radical priests and sisters, the option to join leftist groups was marked by the understanding that solidarity with poor people meant a rejection of capitalism. In making this connection, many sisters, priests, and laypeople joined leftist organizations. For these liberationists, "it was becoming more evident that the Latin American people would not emerge from their present status except by means of a profound transformation, a social revolution that would radically and qualitatively change the conditions in which they lived" (Gutiérrez 1973, 88). They were becoming aware of all that the building of a new society implied, including the possibility that revolutions would force social change and bring about radically altered societies.

The liberation theologians had to ponder what a Marxist religious ethic would mean. This reflection also partly explains why the Catholic right has come to assume that at the heart of liberation is a critique of capitalism with an automatic embrace of socialism. The liberation theologians often turned to the social sciences for their methods of analyses, giving them more opportunities to study the Marxist critique of capitalism. This type of analysis also gave the Catholic right the ammunition it needed to go after the liberation theologians, accusing them of being Marxists and of supporting armed struggles. In fact, one of the earliest weapons in the Catholic right's arsenal was the defection from the priesthood in 1966 of Father Camilo Torres, the Colombian "guerrilla priest" who joined guerrilla forces and was killed in combat.

> Torres was revolutioned by his study of sociology at Louvain. Sociology not only gave him a scientific tool with which to measure the degree of Christian commitment in his country, but also allowed him to see Latin America's economic and political predicament without the rose-colored glasses supplied by Alliance for Progress [the Kennedy administration's economic development plan for Latin America] salespeople. Unlike his classmate Gutiérrez, Torres was a doer, not a thinker, and when all his attempts at peaceful persuasion failed, he shed his cassock to take up arms with the Colombian guerrillas. He died in his first encounter with the Army, on February 15, 1966, in the central Colombian Andes. (Lernoux 1982, 29)

Torres epitomized the extent to which some in the Catholic Church were prepared to engage in Latin America's political struggles, and his actions forced the more liberal sectors of the Church to reexamine the extent of their own commitment to the poor. And by the late 1970s Torres's death, the CELAM conferences (at Medellín, Colombia, in 1968 and at Puebla, Mexico, in 1979), and the burgeoning popularity of liberation theology had impelled significant changes in the Latin American Catholic Church. Many advocates of liberation theology took a less radical stand than Torres but continued to cite their societies' lack of commitment to the poor as a fundamental ethical problem. They questioned the structure of capitalist societies and the resulting economic dependency of third world nations.

The openness to change in the Catholic Church that came with the policies of John XXIII and Paul VI also led to the creation of many forums for the exchange of theological ideas.

The international attention liberation theology received was a consequence of the international Church structure during that period: it nurtured the education of its theologians, facilitated their movement from one country to another, and put at their disposal vast institutional resources. All of that changed, however, with the election in 1978 of Pope John Paul II, a conservative and an advocate of reconciliation as a counter-theme to liberation.

Reconciliation and Sodalitium Vitae

With the support of the new conservatism in the Vatican, the Catholic right in Peru in the 1980s began a formidable challenge against advocates of liberation theology. In their surge to reclaim Church authority, the Catholic right not only prosecuted the opposition by expelling priests, sisters, and a number of Church activists from their parishes but began to push the Church to reject the teaching of liberation theology in seminaries and other Catholic schools. Its greatest triumph has been in organizing conservative movements around the theology of reconciliation.

In Peru the conservative Catholic movement known as Sodalitium Vitae, founded in the early 1970s by a lay Catholic, Luis Fernando Figari, demonstrates the ability of the Catholic right in the 1980s to redirect the protest energy of the 1960s and 1970s into a quieting reformulation of liberation theology as the theology of reconciliation. This shift from concepts of liberation to concepts of reconciliation suggests the limitations of groups that are tied to the same institutional resources as their opponents. Shared institutional ties put protest movements at risk when historical circumstances change in favor of countermovements: hence, the censure, relocation, expulsion, and co-optation of liberation theology by other groups with comparable institutional power.

Figari founded the Sodalitium Vitae movement only three years after Father Gustavo Gutiérrez and others had begun publishing their works on liberation theology, and the theme of reconciliation became the trademark of its campaign against all forms of liberalism and liberationism in the Church. Catholic bishops who supported Sodalitium Vitae assisted the movement when they began using their positions to replace Church personnel and to reorganize parishes wherever they deemed that proponents of liberation theology had "compromised" official Church teachings. At the heart of their dissension was the belief that the theology of liberation, in critiquing the status quo and capitalism, promoted insurrection. Contrary to that belief, I argue that the emergence of the Sodalitium Vitae movement, as well as the reformulation of liberation theology into the theology of reconciliation, is more accurately assessed as an extension of struggles with the popular sector and the polarization created in the Peruvian Church as the Catholic right and left choose sides.

One reason for Sodalitium Vitae's success has been its adherents' ability to link their goals as a movement with a theological perspective attractive to a floating constituency of Church members discontented with liberation theology. It is also true that many who have protested against liberation theology represent the interests of the status quo or of those who believe that even though poverty is a bad thing, the poor do stand to be rewarded in an afterlife for their inconvenience in this one. And although some may argue that advocates of reconciliation are motivated by a sincere commitment to a set of ideals, their attack on liberation theology has nevertheless shaped their political dissonance with the interests of a politically organized popular sector.

Members of the Catholic right have shown their political allegiance on a number of occasions and have never hidden their opposition to liberation theology. As Luis Fernando Fígari wrote: "Progressive theologies absorb the mundane to the point that everything is confused with the religious. Integrationist theologies absorb the religious to the point where everything is confused with the political. For one reason or another, both end in politicizing themselves" (1985, 44). Bishop Ricardo Durand Florez of Callao, Lima, an advocate of Sodalitium Vitae and staunch opponent of liberation theology, has often publicly supported this view:

> When you are concerned with reconciliation you are concerned with the salvific act symbolized by God's saving humanity through the death of his son on the cross, not with political issues. . . .
>
> Now that word, reconciliation, has powerful meaning for our times, as it is directly in opposition to conflict or to Marxist theory, which argues that class conflict is necessary to bring about a just society—a society without classes. Yet conflict can be avoided; if you push yourself to think humanely, you reconcile—each side ceding to the other—and the conflict can be resolved. Marxist theory fuels struggles. . . . In looking to the theology of reconciliation, not only do we reconcile ourselves with God, but we reconcile ourselves with one another. We do not deny that conflict exists, but instead of fueling it, we try to bring solutions. . . .
>
> It is not a reconciliation for fear of what is to come, but because we cannot spend an entire life fighting. . . . It is not to tolerate what is bad, but to fight together against it. Nationally, we could accomplish this, as many groups are doing, such as Sodalitium Vitae. They have a plan in writing, for conferences and other gatherings, carrying and spreading an idea of reconciliation that underscores the Pope's teachings on liberation theology, but in the theology of reconciliation it is to bring out what is logical, correct, and God's work. (1991)

On a similar note, Father Jaime Baertl (1991), a member and spokesperson of the Sodalitium Vitae movement and the organizer of the conferences on reconciliation that have been held in Peru since the mid-1980s, drew an outline of the basic schema of the theology of reconciliation. According to his explanation, it begins with the basic understanding that sin is the root of all evil, and original sin as outlined in the book of Genesis marks the first moment in which people broke their relationship with God. The most fundamental step, then, is to reestablish that relationship. Baertl further explained that here lies the general conflict existent among people. The alienation produced in the moment of breaking with God also produces alienation from oneself, from others, and from nature. The only way to atone or to reorder that which has been put in disorder is to bring about reconciliation. The goal of the theology of reconciliation is to bring back a kind of holistic relationship with God and humanity, which assumes positive effects on the social and economic order of society.

Bishop Oscar Alzamora Revoredo, the former Bishop of Tacna (a coastal city on the border with Chile) and sponsor of one of the first conferences on reconciliation, added his view, which varies slightly:

> In reality, you cannot separate a true theology of liberation from a true theology of reconciliation. These two concepts are not in opposition to each other. When Christ came into the world, he came to liberate and to reconcile. The two are complementary aspects of what represents humanity's state of affairs in the world as a consequence of sin. Therefore, salvation has something to do with both these ideas. Sin enslaves people, and separates them and alienates them from God and others—it alienates people from themselves and from nature. . . . Now what is more important? Well, it depends on what lens you use.
>
> The theme of reconciliation is very important in Peru. But I would not make it, as Baertl's group does, the center of my theology. The center of my theology is grace. It is the grace of the incarnation, the grace of faith, and the grace of redemption. It

is reconciliation, liberation, and many other things. So I would not want to center my theology in this or that idea, no matter how basic or profound it is. . . . In fact, I distrust theologies that make only one central point. What we need is a theology that makes people the center of theology in relation to God with the purpose of saving them, of saving all humanity. (1991)

The ideas shared by Baertl, Alzamora, and other reconciliationists are not really new ideas; in fact, they are extensions of basic official Catholic teachings on social matters. Though one cannot argue that supporters of Sodalitium Vitae are in favor of poverty, they do emphasize patience in enduring poverty and misfortune by focusing on biblical figures who exhibit inexhaustible patience in enduring injustice. The most commonly cited figure is the Virgin Mary, who watched her son unjustly crucified because the end result had some greater purpose: her son's death, according to traditional Christian teachings, proved to be the salvation of humanity.

As Figari has written:

> The young virgin filled with love renounced her comfort, her plans, and plunged herself into what God had in store for her. What a great model for us today who live tied to our small things, who live tied to our plans, our desires, our capriciousness. . . . Mary opted for love. . . . [She is] an example of one who responded to God. . . . In addition, when the moment came for her greatest pain—watching her son crucified—she remained faithful, firm, despite her heart having been pierced by grief. (1985, 138–39)

The use of these biblical images in developing the theology of reconciliation was helpful to opponents of liberation theology at a time when popular insurgency was at its peak in Peru. But it is important to note that the Sodalitium Vitae movement and its theme of reconciliation found allies in other conservative groups—especially Opus Dei—and that that alliance was essential to its mobilizing strategy.

Opus Dei

The Catholic conservative group Opus Dei is important primarily because in Peru it historically preceded Sodalitium Vitae by about twenty years, and during those years a number of its members were named to high-ranking offices within the Catholic Church. In addition, its extensive influence stretches beyond Latin America.

Opus Dei was founded in 1928 by the Spanish priest Josemaría Escrivá de Balaguer y Albás, who conceived the idea during meditation (Vazquez De Prada 1984, 16). In 1933, with only a few followers, Escrivá opened the DYA Academy (Academy for Law and Architecture). The organization's name later has been attributed to a friend's inquiry to Escrivá: "How is your God's work progressing?" (Le Tourneau 1986, 14). Since then, it has been known as Opus Dei, derived from the Latin *operatio Dei,* meaning "God's work." Opus Dei leaders eventually moved their headquarters from Spain to Rome—a strategic move, some critics have charged, because is allowed the leadership to influence decisions at the Vatican.

Escrivá's *Camino,* the "bible" of Opus Dei teachings, has sold more than three million copies in thirty-five languages. In Peru, for example, it has been translated into Quechua, an enterprise aimed at reaching indigenous and Andean peasants. Opus Dei has an extensive international information and publication network. Many of its books are published in Spain by the editorial house Ediciones Rialp in Madrid, and other publications are initiated in Rome, but wherever the organization has expanded, it has founded local dissemination networks. In Peru there are Editorial Antonio Lulli in Lima and Editorial Andina in Cusco.

The Opus Dei movement established itself in Peru in 1955 in the province of Yauyos. From the beginning, it mirrored the earlier influx of certain traditional missionaries—the type that has imposed a conservative religious pattern on Latin America. The Opus Dei Spanish leadership sent to establish, organize, and operate projects for Peruvians, reflected this attitude. Among the first to arrive was Bishop Ignacio Maria de Orbegozzo—who later became Archbishop of Chiclayo, a coastal city north of Lima—and at least nine women were sent to organize women's centers. Subsequently, Father Vicente Pazos became Conciliario (the highest ranking adviser); Luis Tejerizo was put in charge of the women's sector, and Father Antonio Ducay became their spiritual director; Father Ramon Rocca Salles became director of the seminary in Chiclayo. All these officials came from Spain; in fact, a look at the 1987 Church directory for Peru (*Directorio* 1987) confirms that the Opus Dei leadership in Peru was an imported one from the start.

According to one priest who asked to remain anonymous, the arrangement of key ecclesial positions was established early in Peru's Opus Dei history. Rome's nuncio at the time (the official Vatican representative to the region) assigned the care of the Prelature of Cañete first to Bishop Orbegozzo in 1963, and then to Bishop Sanchez-Moreno Lira in 1968, when Orbegozzo became Bishop of Chiclayo. These arrangements gave Opus Dei two major ecclesial strongholds and were the culmination of what some perceived as the organization's expansion in Peru.

That expansion included the University of Piura, which was built with funds raised by Opus Dei's Asociación para el Desarrollo de la Enseñanza Universitaria (ADEU), or the Association for the Advancement of University Teaching. A pamphlet distributed by the University of Piura reported donations by "Friends of the University" as follows: 51.06 percent from Lima, 20.42 percent from Piura, none from other areas of Peru, and 1.35 percent from abroad (sources of the remaining

27.17 percent were not specified). These statistics reveal two important points: first, the financial support for the university came mostly from within Peru; second, the major source was Lima. Apparently, Opus Dei's main resource center was Lima, and other assistance was supplied by local, wealthy Opus Dei laypeople. It is interesting to note that no income came from other Peruvian provinces, suggesting that Opus Dei's influence in Peru, though strong, is limited.

According to an interview with Bishop Alvaro del Portillo y Díez de Sollano, the organization's president-general, as of 1984 Opus Dei claimed more than 74,000 members in forty-two countries (Kamm 1984). Of these, 30,000 were committed to a celibate life-style, even though most of these members were laypeople; only 2 percent were reported to be priests. Opus Dei's secrecy policy has made it difficult for outsiders to get accurate statistics, but it has been estimated that South American bishops who are members include at least three in Peru, one in Ecuador, and one in Venezuela, and the 1987 Peruvian ecclesial directory listed twenty priests as members.

Opus Dei's identity was shaped at a time when the main quarrel in the Church was "between intransigent Catholics and anticlerical liberals of 19th century vintage. The quarrel was sharpened by the Spanish Civil War (1936–1939), which Escrivá regarded as a crusade against the hordes of godlessness. He urged his followers to patriotism: to be Catholic means to love your country and to be second to no one in that love" (Hebblethwaite 1983, 9).

In living out their founder's vision, the members of Opus Dei try to cultivate the spirit of sacrifice as a way to purify themselves in order to "secure true and lasting spiritual development, so as to prepare themselves for the Apostolate . . . and to show their love for Christ, who chose to die on the cross for the love of humanity" (Le Tourneau 1986, 138). They see the poor as privileged because they are in good positions to reenact the suffering of Jesus Christ on the cross in their everyday lives. They can also offer their pain as a way of achieving spiritual perfection, which is the underlying goal of each Opus Dei member—although critics have charged that it is part of the Opus Dei strategy to quiet political dissent, particularly among the poor. For that reason and because it has taken actions against political protest, Opus Dei is often accused of serving the interest of the political right.

Certainly, Opus Dei has been useful to the Catholic right in Peru, because it is in the battle against liberation theology and has put its resources behind that endeavor. It's Peruvian journal *Antología de Textos,* for example, often features articles on traditional Catholic values and scathing condemnations of liberation theology. Another asset in Peru has been the University of Piura's ADEU press; in its Collección Algarrobo series, ADEU listed as its director Professor Luz Gonzalez Umeres, a principal figure in Peru's women's sector of Opus Dei. The university claims complete independence but its resources, personnel, and religious instruction are guided by Opus Dei.

Other organizational assets in Peru are the Opus Dei cultural centers, which nurture what some describe as "valuable social links." An informant who asked not to be identified explained: "Students often study in Opus Dei centers, because they provide a pleasant social environment. Often the invitations to visit one of the centers come from another friend, already an Opus Dei follower, who has been pressed to bring in potential new recruits." And according to the same informant, Opus Dei always stresses to its followers the importance of attracting recruits who have certain qualities:

> They had to be able to create an atmosphere of family life, couldn't have physical handicaps, had to be joyful, pious, studi-

ous—this they took into account later; it wasn't the most important thing at first. More important was their social and economic status. They had to come from "good" backgrounds. I feel the latter was most important. The comments that were circulated were that . . . [new members] had to come from the best in society, so as to influence society from the top. Later it seemed that it became more difficult to recruit women from good economic backgrounds, so they began to admit women of lower economic status, so long as they were university students or offered other possibilities for Opus Dei.

Lower-class women filled low positions in the Opus Dei organization: they became servants who, according to another informant,

> were called "auxiliary numeraries." They worked in the kitchen, participated in farming or the printing presses of Opus Dei. They were never alone—always accompanied by numeraries. They had separate bedrooms, smaller than the rooms of the numeraries. And they were treated like children, so they often acted extremely childish.
>
> [The women from the lower classes], for example, felt very attracted [to Opus Dei] because of the way the numeraries treated them; they created a family atmosphere. They were very simple people, coming as they did from extreme poverty. Many of them had worked since they were small, in the markets and as *ambulantes* [street vendors]. . . . Therefore, arriving at a place that offered to give you your own room, with abundant numbers of bathrooms around, and getting sanitary food was very attractive to them. . . . These women [who worked on the Condoray Project in Cañete, a rural town two hours south of Lima] wanted to have a career in the hotel industry at the middle levels, even though this program essentially prepared them to work as maids.

The Condoray Project is an Opus Dei vocational center for peasant women which encourages development among the rural communities in the vicinity of Cañete. The work there also includes a variety of agricultural programs, which teach women the development, maintenance, and care of their own vegetable gardens. Part of Opus Dei's goal is to teach peasants how to be self-sufficient. Thus, it runs a food program for children with the purpose of instructing mothers about child nutrition, and teaching the children tasks they can perform in their homes when they return to their communities. Cañete provides three medical facilities as well, where peasants can receive medical attention and information about basic health care. Other projects include water purification, instruction in labor skills, stock raising, training in health and nutrition, and the organization of recreational competitions and folklore festivals. Overall, the Cañete programs provide services to twelve villages.

Since the Catholic Church, as stated in their promotional brochure, has charged Opus Dei with the responsibility of spiritual and doctrinal formation in Cañete, Opus Dei university students are encouraged to give their time to work in these rural communities. One informant commented: "We teach women things that have to do with the house and their children. For the children, we make toys from whatever you find in the community. We teach them to make the best of what they have." And because of the successes people see in Cañete, many, including nonmembers, support Opus Dei.

Other cultural centers in Peru have been established under the names Tángara, Altozano, Puhira, Miralba (a house for the directorship of the women's sector), Los Andes (which fulfills the same function for men), and the University of Piura, where there are dorms and study centers for men and women. In Lima, there are the Salcantay, Alpamajo, Altea, and Saeta elementary schools. Additional establishments include Montemar, an institute for the study of graphic design, and Alcabor, which provides training for teachers, nurses, social workers, and so on. All these centers and projects are designed to attract new recruits among students, young professionals, and persons from the upper classes—recruits who can make Opus Dei politically influential.

Clearly, though a total assessment of its networking potential in Peru is difficult because of the group's secrecy about its activities, Opus Dei controls a wide array of resources and exercises extensive influence in the Latin American Catholic Church. Opponents of the organization have expressed the fear that if it goes unchallenged, Opus Dei could succeed in overrunning the priesthood and the Peruvian hierarchy with its own personnel; they see the lack of free speech and tight rein over parish activities in Chiclayo, for example, as the model that Opus Dei would apply to the rest of Peru. Others fear that Opus Dei priests and officials are already in key positions and located where they can exercise extensive influence over the Peruvian hierarchy. In any case, by putting their organizational resources behind Sodalitium Vitae, these influential officials are well able to strengthen the Catholic right's campaign against liberation theology.

Summary
In Latin America, liberation theology has carried with it all the characteristics of a dynamic religious movement. Latin American priests, theologians, and other religious intellectuals used their skills, resources, and networks to promote political movements and, in so doing, transformed the very institution that formed them. But although the theme of liberation became the basis for reform and social change in the Latin Amerian Church, traditionalism became the trademark of such organizations within the Church as Opus Dei and Sodalitium Vitae. The coexistence of liberation theology with these organizations mirrors the complexity of the Catholic Church in Peru. The dynamic adversarial interaction created by these

conflicting ideas and strategies provides an ideal locus for analyzing the intricacies of social movement mobilization and of the social forces involved in the recruitment of religious intellectuals to social causes.

The Catholic Church, as an institution of power bound to both national and international constituencies, has proved a testing ground for the way intellectuals use their skills to garner institutional support for one group or another. Some historical periods provide a climate conducive to any number of different mobilization efforts; other periods, characterized by repression, apathy, or complacency, are inhospitable to such efforts (Gamson 1988, 223). In Latin America, religious congregations and influential cardinals and bishops have provided leverage for hosting international conferences on theology and sometimes served as a bridge between the Vatican and the Latin American theologians themselves. Each side has used these forums to advance its own movement. Without some of this key support, liberation theology and its theologians would have been limited to local sponsorship and more vulnerable to local censure; international forums, however, boosted the networks of local groups. This mobilization phenomenon has depended on some individuals who were enabled to articulate certain collective visions that, in the case of liberation theology, went beyond the scope of the institutional Catholic Church's intentions, forcing opponents to couch their attack in careful language about what aspects of liberation theology the Church finds unacceptable.

Sociologists have only recently engaged in studies of the importance of political discourse in the arsenal of mobilization processes. Compelling ideologies, an organized constituency, effective leadership, and a people joined by common goals can both mobilize and sustain mass protest. Learning how these factors come together to form effective protest is the key to understanding broader issues in resource mobilization. Religious leaders, their ideas, and other church constituencies become resources that can be mobilized at a time of crisis. Critical to this process are individuals who are able to assess strategies and act accordingly. The motivation to act often comes from a belief that real change can occur only through action. The expression of those beliefs is often the main focus of study, assuming that mobilization occurs because a group believes in a cause. But I propose that intellectuals and the ideologies they profess can play a greater role in social movements than simply creating beliefs in causes; they often become the underlying reason for network development and constituency overlap.

In analyzing the ways Peruvian theologians and other intellectuals managed their organizational resources, this book uncovers a key link between Church activists who supported popular protest, Church intellectuals who articulated the religious justification for their struggles, and a Church structure that for a time supported and increased possibilities for popular activism. Central to this process were other populations and other networks that became useful to the causes of the poor because some liberation theologians effectively articulated the ideological overlaps that existed among all the constituencies involved.

In the field of sociology, resource mobilization theories have successfully identified the material conditions that underlie the emergence of social movements. These theories tend to emphasize the importance of material resources—that is, the ability to finance activities—and organizational resources such as membership, newsletters, and linkage to other networks. What resource mobilization theorists must now consider is which—and why—ideological constructs become crucial components of social movement strategies that also help in the mobilization process. It is in identifying the relationship between ideological factors and social movements that resource mobilization theory has been negligent. (Snow and Benford 1988, 197–98).

This book attempts to contribute to that growing literature by showing that liberationist priests, bishops, and theologians—in concert with an already organized and active population—engaged in exchanges that facilitated the development of a broad spectrum of networks and resources, primarily because their ideological positions resonated with the popular sector. The ability to generate a set of ideas compelling to more than one population can become a critical factor in social movement mobilization processes.

Today, no one can deny that in Peru and the rest of Latin America theology has played an important role in articulating for religious men and women theological rationales for becoming politically active. More important, theology has provided the ideological basis for a religious constituency's justification of its political activities. But the translation and adaptation of religious principles, making them relevant to social action, has depended on the interpretive skills of ministers and theologians who can translate for their community the ideals of the group. Similarly, the Sodalitium Vitae movement has succeeded in generating institutional support by framing the theology of reconciliation discourse as an alternative to liberation theology. One central reason for Sodalitium Vitae's success has been its ability to link its goals as a movement with a theological perspective attractive to a floating constituency of Church members who have become discontented with liberation theology—including, in Peru, followers of Opus Dei.

Whether priests and missionaries become conservative or liberal proponents of change depends on the specific social forces at work. Conservative bishops and priests in Peru, for example, in concert with an organized and active population—the Sodalitium Vitae movement—facilitated the development of outside networks and the pooling of resources. Like the liberationist, they were able to mobilize influential Church leaders and disseminate information through conferences at national and international levels. Mobilizing these resources made them better able to promote a social movement program in line with traditional Church social teachings, and to go after what they perceived to be the breakdown of traditional values and hierarchical authority.

The resurgence of traditionalism in Latin America, the emergence of a co-optive ideology (the theology of reconciliation), and a regrouping of conservatives not only undermined liberationist ideology but also paralleled the expulsion and censure of a number of groups professing to be advocates of liberation theology. That turn of events, primarily in the 1980s, led to a general reorganization of experimental communities and other projects created during the liberalization of the Church that began in the early 1960s. A central point to be argued in this regard is that both liberation theology and its conservative opposition in the Peruvian Catholic Church emerged within Latin America's larger political struggles.

Thus, the overarching argument in this book is that changes in historical circumstances have shaped the content and discourse of theology in Peru and Latin America. Before any analysis of the liberation theology debate can take place, therefore, an overview of Catholic Church history is necessary—particularly the history behind the power struggles that occurred in the 1980s and 1990s and allowed the Sodalitium Vitae movement and the theology of reconciliation to come to the forefront in the Church's confrontation with liberation theology. Peru serves as a case study both of why liberation theology is so popular and of why it has come under attack.

CHAPTER TWO

The Catholic Church in Peru

One thing is clear: the Catholic Church's hold on the educational and cultural institutions of Latin America during and after the colonization period has thus far produced five centuries of a predominantly Catholic mind-set that has influenced every aspect of Latin American society. The period of independence only solidified the Church's control over the cultural development of the Spanish- and Portuguese-appropriated lands. By the nineteenth century the Catholic Church had achieved its establishment as a political force in each Latin American country and, with the infusion of Catholicism as the dominant religion, a guaranteed influence over the intellectual development of its people.

Many Latin American countries have gone so far as to guarantee the Church special legal privileges, often written into their constitutions. For example, the Peruvian constitutions (with only slight modifications) have declared Roman Catholicism the state religion. And only the 1979 constitutional revision altered church-state relations by limiting the Church to a more collaborative, rather than an authoritarian, role in matters of education and health. This history is important to an understanding of the significance of liberation theology, particularly for Peruvians. How and why Father Gustavo Gutiérrez came to produce his brand of liberation theology is reflected in the history of the Catholic Church in Latin America.

The Catholic Church came to the Western Hemisphere as part of the colonial machinery that changed the Americas forever, and some of Latin America's well-known reformers and revolutionaries have been products of Catholic education and social reform programs. But colonial history also reflects the fact that indigenous peoples and their descendants have resisted the colonization process. Some have argued that though European rule in the region devastated the indigenous communities, colonial institutions such as the Catholic Church were themselves marked by the experiences. In fact, whereas Catholic kings had a politics of military expansion, economic mercantilism, and evangelization by which they proposed to unify Europe and the world within the Roman Catholic Church under the sign of the cross, the missionary Church sometimes opposed this state of affairs. From the onset of Latin America's colonial history, despite the fact that widespread injustice was extremely difficult to uproot, nearly everything positive that was done for the benefit of the indigenous peoples resulted from the call and clamor of some missionaries (Dussel 1981, 45). Priests such as Bartolomé de Las Casas, who served as Bishop of Chiapas, Mexico (1544–47), Antonio de Valdivieso of Nicaragua, Fernando de Uranga of Cuba, Vasco de Quiroga of Mexico, and many others became voices of protest against the injustices inflicted on Latin America's indigenous peoples. Research into the lives of these missionaries has shown that they "risked everything, committing themselves without reservation, suffering expulsion from their dioceses, imprisonment, deportation, and even death on behalf of the Native Americans who were being violently oppressed and exploited by the Spanish colonists" (Dussel 1981, 51).

In many ways, these missionaries' style of protest and the price they paid for it foreshadows the experience of liberation theologians and their adherents. The history of the emergence of liberation theology reflects the complex pattern of protest that has characterized Latin American Church history. Any understanding of liberation theology requires an analysis of Latin America's church-state relations.

The Colonial Scene

In 1492 Columbus and Catholicism landed in the Americas, and by the late sixteenth century the Catholic Church had officially established itself by setting up three branches of the Inquisition's Tribunal: in Peru, Mexico, and Colombia. This court, which was established by the Catholic Church in the thirteenth century for the discovery and suppression of heresy, also went after those believed to be dangerous to the ruling powers, and its Latin American branches followed this pattern. Their early mission was characterized by two main endeavors: the Church hierarchy's acceptance and advancement of political rule by the colonists; and the institutionalization of papal pronouncements that gave the Catholic Church exclusive control over the evangelization of Native Americans as colonized subjects of the Iberian kings. During the colonial period the papacy ceded to the Iberian crowns the "right and responsibility," the *jus patronatus,* of propagating the faith among peoples in newly discovered lands (Dussel 1981, 38). It was the first time in history that the papacy had granted a state the twofold authority to colonize and to evangelize. In other words, the Church gave the colonizing states in Latin America temporal and eternal, political and ecclesiastical, economic and evangelistic authority.

This papal action united the interests and aspirations of the Iberian kings and the Church. Together they were responsible for the exploitation and suppression of Latin America's indigenous population and culture, and the systematic imposition of a Catholic value system and world view. The result was centuries of almost exclusive Catholic influence over the lives and cultures of Latin Americans. The success of this campaign is reflected in the estimate that 90 percent of Latin Americans today baptize their children Roman Catholic.

The colonial missionary drive was so efficient that according to the Peruvian historian Ruben Ugarte, art, music, and theater made Catholic ideology accessible, clear, and easy to understand not only in Peru but throughout Latin America (1953, 325). Everywhere in Latin America the Catholic Church mobilized to promote the Christian ethic of the colonizers, leading to the virtual extinction of the religions of the indigenous peoples.

The power of the Inquisition's Tribunal made the drive more effective. The list of responsibilities the Tribunal assigned itself included press censorship, punishment of misconduct among the clergy and violations of Catholic dogma, and the establishment of rules to guard against threats to Catholicism from other faiths—particularly by limiting the number of Jews who could emigrate to the "new world." Through the Tribunal's actions, the Church established control over secular as well as religious activities, placing key institutions under the exclusive control of Roman Catholic governance. The Inquisition consolidated and exercised authority in all matters related to the Spanish colonies: religious, economic, administrative, political, and military (Dussel 1981, 38). Its laws protected and enforced Catholic norms well into the beginning of the period of Latin American independence movements. The Iberian kings and the Roman Catholic Church consolidated socioeconomic power by dismantling indigenous societies and superseding them with those of the colonists. And through a variety of legal mechanisms that the Iberian crowns ensured, the Church established in Latin America the political, cultural, and ideological dominance that it has exercised ever since.

The Church mirrored and crystallized the Spanish and Portuguese colonial system, which destroyed the various Andean structural networks and superseded and consolidated power through such systems as *reducciones,* or reductions. These, from the earliest times of the Spanish conquest, involved the gathering and unifying of Native Americans into types of communities that such bishops as Vasco de Quiroga and Bartolomé de Las Casas considered humane and the only effective means of civilizing and evangelizing them (Dussel 1981, 344). For the most part, however, the reductions benefited the colonists and the Church, for the religious instruction of Native Americans was coupled with the labor extracted from them. Some have argued that in the sixteenth century the priest Bartolomé de Las Casas (the champion of indigenous causes at the time) and others used the reductions to try to protect and promote the rights of Native Americans. Some still argue that the system was a good one because it offered an alternative to the brutal exploitation of Native Americans at the hands of greedy speculators. Others, however, assert that it simply produced a different type of indigenous annihilation: little by little the Native American communities, deprived of the ultimate bases of their cultures, began to adopt the culture of the Spanish (Dussel 1981, 66).

In an interview, Maryknoll sister Rosa Dominga Trapasso, cofounder of the feminist Christian Talitha Cumi organization (based in Lima), who has worked in Peru for more than twenty-five years, commented that over the centuries "the Church has seen itself as power, control, paternalistic, and the poor as dependent on her as dutiful sons and daughters" (1988). So not only did the Iberian invasion and conquest lead to the disintegration of Native American life and culture, but it replaced them with a Catholic mind-set such that indigenous peoples, their cultures, and religious beliefs became the marginal elements of the new society. And this, through the centuries, produced a type of dependency.

With the coming of independence in the early 1800s, the Catholic Church had so effectively established and promoted Portuguese and Spanish culture that Catholicism was made the official state religion in practically every Latin American country and was thus able to influence legislation on divorce and other legal matters. In Peru, for example, little was lost to the Catholic Church, because the new political leadership immediately compensated those members of the lower clergy who had shown sympathy toward the pro-independence forces (Astiz 1969, 168). The new authorities maintained that they had inherited the right, formerly granted to the Spanish crown, to appoint the clergy. And all appointments, promotions, and transfers were to be filled with patriotic priests. The Church thus accommodated the new political situation by aligning itself with the new elites.

Political Movements against the Church in Peru

After the achievement of independence in Peru, the Catholic Church came to be viewed as one of the new nation's four powerful political entities; the others were the military, the state, and the national elites. For the indigenous peoples and the mestizos (persons of mixed Native American and Spanish descent), independence meant only the beginning of a different kind of subjugation: instead of being exploited (in tribute, labor, and land), by the colonizers, they would become dominated by the *criollos,* or creoles (American-born descendants of the Spanish). Many indigenous communities had fought for independence with the promise that they would no longer have to pay tribute and could look forward to sharing equally in the new society. But the republic that Peru became in the nineteenth century did not erase the chasm that ultimately gave the *criollos* a distinct advantage over the indigenous and mestizo peoples (Soriano 1985, 225–27).

By the end of the nineteenth century, Peru had begun to build itself as an independent nation in which the dominant classes were exercising their influence as urban capitalists, as landed aristocrats *(hacendados),* and as entrepreneurs in commerce and mining (Matos Mar 1987, 28); foreign investment helped them accumulate significant wealth. With the growth of capitalism, scores of salaried workers emerged and by the early 1920s were populating the coastal cities of Peru in significant numbers. In areas dominated by agricultural capital investments, however, peasants lost their property and became slaves, in effect, to the *enganche,* or hook, which kept peasants legally bound to the *patrones* of *haciendas:* that is, the landed aristocracy. Under this system, in exchange for food, clothing, and housing, peasants agreed to work for minimal wages, which were often reclaimed as payment for merchandise or services that were not part of their working contracts. Thus, the expansion of the *latifundia* (landed estates) system and capital investment developed a new form of political hegemony: indigenous peoples and peasants who had been dominated under colonialism remained dominated in the new republics by expanding capitalism.

Eventually, this growing exploitation led to the formation of peasant- and worker-based movements and, in more extreme circumstances, to revolutions. During the early 1920s in Peru, two important figures emerged: José Carlos Mariategui, an avowed Marxist-Leninist and founder of the first of the leftist organizations that eventually formed under the banner of Izquierda Unida (IU), or the United Left; and Victor Raúl Haya de la Torre, founder of the Alianza Popular Revolucionaria Americana (APRA), or the American Popular Revolutionary Alliance. Together, Mariategui and Haya de la Torre constructed the foundation on which social protest would be based: mobilization against oligarchy and imperialism, with an orientation toward the political participation of the popular and middle urban sectors (Cotler 1987, 201–4). APRA, for example, envisioned five basic goals: the fight against U.S. imperialism, political unification of Latin America, nationalization of property and industry, internationalization of the Panama Canal, and solidary actions with oppressed peoples and classes everywhere, including those involved in armed struggles.

In Mariategui's view, the independence movement in Latin America, and Peru in particular, had not been the product of an organic bourgeoisie, nor did it inspire the formation of a bourgeoisie with a vocation toward revolution capable of destroying its feudal ties (Cotler 1987, 217). Rather, from the moment Peru became a republic, the inheritors of the colonial nobility quickly transformed themselves into intermediaries of the European capitalism that at the time dominated the Peruvian economy. Eventually, U.S. interests came into play, as well. As for the Catholic Church, both Mariategui and Haya de la Torre came to see it as being on the side of local elites, who often cast their lot with foreign investors without regard to what that would mean to workers, peasants, and the poor of their country.

No hostility toward the Catholic Church was expressed more fiercely than by followers of Sendero Luminoso (SL), or the Shining Path, an offshoot of Peru's Communist Party (PCP). "Rebel graffiti up and down the country articulated the tenor of Sendero Luminoso's plans for the Church: slogans gleefully announced that the revolution would have it for 'pudding'" (Strong 1992, 175). As Father Gustavo Gutiérrez has observed, Ayacucho, a southern mountain region of Peru and the birthplace of the Shining Path, was a weak point in the Peruvian Church, "probably because [the bishop] wanted to preserve certain customs and privileges and feared losing them by being stronger and more energetic in the face of repressive violence. . . . In failing to defend the population or recognize the roots of subversion, the Church hierarchy in Ayacucho divorced itself from the poor and contributed to the power vacuum filled by Shining Path" (quoted in Strong 1992, 174).

The history of Sendero Luminoso began in 1964 when the Peruvian Communist Party divided into pro-Soviet and pro-Chinese factions. The PCP local of Ayacucho aligned itself with the latter, which came to be called the PCP–Bandera Roja (PCP–Red Flag). Almost from the start, a small group within the Red Flag organization banded around Abimael Guzmán and eventually split from Bandera Roja to form the PCP-Sendero Luminoso (PCP-SL) in the latter half of 1969 or early 1970 (Degregori 1990, 18). At this early date Sendero Luminoso was still ten years away from declaring itself a guerrilla revolutionary movement. In July 1980, however, they did so by initiating a series of bombings in Ayacucho and by using graffiti on walls, calling all Peruvians to join the "popular war." With that declaration came what some have called Sendero's reign of terror. Yet even its critics would agree that the emergence of SL's guerrilla movement and the resulting spotlight of publicity forced Peruvians to take notice of the harsh realities of Peru's poor and the social conditions that had led to the rise and spread of Sendero Luminoso.

The Catholic Church had to face the fact that it had had

something to do with advancing the marginality of Ayacuchanos and other neglected citizens. For centuries, no one had
taken up the indigenous cause, nor had the Church put itself
at the forefront of dissent over Peru's neglect of Ayacucho and
other regions like it. A hands-off stance had been the primary
position of the institutional Church. Only with the development of liberation theology was there any real systematic critique of that indifferent attitude. But by the time liberation
theology really started to take hold among the more politicized sectors of the Church, Sendero Luminoso had already
made its mark on the region. Because for centuries the Catholic Church, as one of Peru's most powerful institutional forces,
had sided with the ruling classes, for the Peruvian left it was a
mere extension of Peru's hegemonic forces. And when liberation theologians emerged as an anomaly to that history, the
more radical left had become overtly anti-Church.

The history of Sendero Luminoso is the history of Peru's
class struggles coming to a head. The rise of Sendero Luminoso can be partly explained by the influence of the intellectual vanguard that came to control the University of Hua-
manga in Ayacucho (Degregori 1990, 16–17); the other half
of the story focuses on Peru's economic and political abandon-
ment of its provinces, a policy that disproportionately affected
Ayacucho through the 1980s. Capitalist development and im-
perialist penetration from the nineteenth century into the
twentieth century, very clearly affected Ayacucho in negative
ways (Degregori 1990, 28). The region possessed few or no
resources of interest to national or international investors, nor
did there exist an economic center sufficiently thriving to lure
business from the more prosperous parts of the country.

In sum, the disintegration of the region of Ayacucho was
marked by a stagnant economy with little prospect for investment, and like other regions of the sierras and the Amazon

basin, it suffered the neglect of an economically and politically centralized government whose decision-making occurred entirely in Peru's capital city, Lima. As one merchant from Ayacucho, interviewed in 1936, complained: "Today Ayacucho is uninhabited and in absolute economic decay, because there is a shortage of jobs for workers, [who] thus have to migrate to the coast in search of work, while the rich families of the region come to Lima living off their rents" (quoted in Degregori 1990, 29). The pattern has changed very little since then. Between 1876 and 1940 the capital city of the Department of Ayacucho (also named Ayacucho), compared with eleven other sierra capital cities, recorded the slowest rate of economic growth. And between 1940 and 1961 it surpassed only Pasco, a region of the sierras north of Ayacucho and east of Lima today, the Departments of Ayacucho and Apurimac rank highest on "Peru's Map of Poverty." Of the country's ten poorest provinces in 1990, three were in Huancavelica and two in Ayacucho: Cangallo placed second and Victor Fajardo placed seventh, precisely the provinces where Sendero's armed struggle initiated in 1980 (Degregori 1990, 29, 32).

Throughout the 1960s the Catholic Church together with the traditional landed elites "seemed to maintain a conservative political hegemony in much of the area"; in fact, when union organizers and Marxist political leaders sought to mobilize peasants in the highland regions, *hacienda* authorities identified them quickly and barred them from the vicinity (McClintock 1989, 71). This historical reality explains in part why Sendero was able not only to gain popularity in that region but to spread to other regions. The SL emerged at a time very propitious for protest in Ayacucho's history and did well in deprived areas. The region had grown increasingly hostile toward the landed elites, and peasants were beginning to express dissatisfaction with Peru's social inequities. According to the political scientist Cynthia McClintock (1989, 67), in the early 1980s peasants in Peru's southern highlands faced what was possibly the most serious threat to their subsistence of the twentieth century. As living standards plummeted throughout the nation, in Ayacucho, Apurimac, and Huanca-velica, where living standards were already much lower than in the rest of the country, the decline meant virtual starvation. At the same time, as the literacy rate in the region began to increase and more Ayacuchanos gained access to education, the knowledge about their status in Peru and some of the reasons for it became clearer, Sendero simply sparked flame where revolt was already smoldering.

The rise of Sendero also sharpened divisions between progressive, radical, conservative, and traditionalist Catholics, particularly as they confronted the crises brought on by civil war. These divisions in the Church were reflected in different attitudes toward human rights abuses. Although the official position was to condemn them unequivocally, the ultraconservatives uttered hardly a word of protest and in some cases, notably in Ayacucho, moved to prevent denunciations against security forces (Strong 1992, 168–69). On the other side were those who condemned the abuses and, though not supporting Sendero, were clearly on the side of other peasant movements. Among the more visible were those who supported the principles of the theology of liberation.

Focusing on the Church in Latin America only in terms of its relation with the status quo, however, presents a distorted view of Catholic history in the region. Though it is true that the Church has tended to align itself with political and economic elites in Latin America, its role in Peru extends beyond this simple conclusion. Despite the indictments that can be made against the Catholic Church in Peru, other facts have to be considered. For example, at the same time that many of

Peru's elites were emerging as products of prestigious Catholic schools, so too were some of the Church's strongest opponents and the country's most radical reformers—including Sendero Luminoso's idol, Abimael Guzmán. Though Guzmán ultimately denounced the Catholic Church, he too had attended Catholic schools in Arequipa, an economically and politically stable sierra city to the south of Ayacucho. So had supporters of liberation theology, some of them from rich families, though adherents of liberation theology have never supported Sendero Luminoso.

Many of Father Gutiérrez's strongest supporters were members of the United Left, an umbrella organization representing Peru's leftist parties. Sendero, in splitting from the PCP, also split from IU, making clear that it had no place for Peru's parliamentary left. The Catholic right, however, has used Sendero's guerrilla activities to denounce liberation theology. Looking for opportunities to implicate supporters of liberation theology in radical leftist activities, it tried to use the fact that some liberationists backed the Sandinistas in Nicaragua, the national liberation movement (FMLN) in El Salvador, and the guerrilla groups of the ex-priest Camilo Torres in Colombia. And even though supporters of liberation theology in Peru have denounced Sendero Luminoso, they have been tagged as suspect. Some members of the Catholic right focused on Edmundo Cox Beuzeville, the son of a devout Catholic, upper-class Peruvian family, who was implicated in subversive activities in 1981. Others noted that several former nuns had joined Sendero Luminoso—among them Nelly Evans, who was married for a short time to Carlos Alvarez Calderón, the brother of Jorge Alvarez Calderón, a cornerstone of the Catholic worker movement; Evans's association with Carlos cast suspicion on both brothers. In the eyes of the Catholic right, the Alvarez Calderón brothers were already suspect because they were involved in fighting for workers' rights, and any support of workers, land squatters, or poor people's movements in general meant that the participants had become politicized. Because of the Alvarez Calderóns' very clear commitment to working with the poor and advocating their rights, the Catholic right labeled them radicals.

By the late 1970s the Catholic right had begun its targeted campaign against insurgency, against political activism, and against liberation theology. Again, however, it is important to note the irony that the same Church structure produced both those aligned with Peru's political elites *and* their opponents: people like Gutiérrez, the Alvarez Calderón brothers, and others—often from privileged backgrounds—who supported the poor.

The Influence of Catholic Action

In the late nineteenth century, Catholic congregations of sisters and priests arrived in Peru to replenish the dwindling number of religious congregations that had established themselves in the colonial period. The Sisters of Charity of Saint Vincent de Paul were assigned to establish and maintain hospitals in Lima. Two congregations from France—the Redemptionists and the Religious of the Sacred Heart—took up missionary activities in Lima, Junin, Huancavelica, Ayacucho, and Apurimac. The latter established most of their work in Lima. The Jesuits, another Sacred Heart congregation, and the Salesians all arrived soon afterward. Together, these groups influenced the social and intellectual world of Peru by establishing prestigious high schools and the Pontifical Catholic University of Lima, schools that have produced many influential political figures in both conservative and liberal camps (Ugarte 1962, 239).

These schools also provided an institutional context in

which theological ideas and various Church movements found access to like-minded individuals and to potential recruits. Such access is especially important in a context where movements try to build coalition strategies and "attempt to mobilize ideological commitments held by members of already existing groups" (Ferree and Miller 1985, 49). Among these existing groups was the Catholic Action movement, which had been germinating since the late nineteenth century in Europe. The mass dislocation of European workers due to industrialization had forced many in the Church to question the social implications of unbridled capitalism. This moment in history created the space for the development of new Catholic social thought, which was manifested as Catholic Action.

Catholic Action was important to the eventual development of liberation theology because it set the precedent for supporting workers' rights and critiquing capitalism. Although the movement ebbed somewhat during the 1920s, Catholic Action experienced a kind of rebirth during the Great Depression, when the issues again focused on workers, their plight, and their demands for a fair distribution of wealth. Debate during these two periods sparked two encyclicals (open letters from the pope to Catholics). The second of these, "Quadragesimo Anno" (After forty years), was issued by Pope Pius XI in 1931, on the fortieth anniversary of the first: "Rerum Novarum" (1891), in which Leo XIII had discussed the problems of workers as a fundamental social issue.

Although both encyclicals were written with the intent of arousing sentiment against labor exploitation and class division, they were firm in their condemnation of socialism as a possible solution to the problems. And even though for some this antisocialist stance was limiting, many in the Church saw the documents' usefulness as advancing the interests of union labor. Others, however, wanted the Church to push for economic systems that were based on classless societies. While the antisocialist stance brought on debate in the Church, all agreed that at minimum the encyclicals extolled the ideal of social justice for the common good of all, by which the popes meant the good or welfare of all persons and classes within any given community (Abell 1963, 239). In the end, many Catholics, driven by the call for social justice, joined the Catholic Action movement as advocates of even greater social reform than the encyclicals promoted.

As the Depression infused the Catholic Action movement with new life in many countries, "liberal Catholics throughout the U.S. interpreted the 1931 encyclical as a mandate for involvement with social problems, and they quickly moved to the fore in many areas of the Church. . . . Taking control of existing publications or establishing new ones, they made Catholic periodicals into forceful advocates of reform" (Brinkley 1983, 129). This kind of control is a significant feature of social movement activities, because social movement researchers have found that organizational networks and newspapers, as well as material resources, are important to the success of such movements. Catholic Action proved useful to Catholic political activists because of its importance as a training ground (Whyte 1981, 86). Its members developed skills in administration, public speaking, and the conciliation of differences, all of which proved valuable to politicians during elections and in their efforts to rally people to their causes.

The argument here again underscores the importance of analyzing ideology with the sociohistorical milieu of movement participants. The connectedness of movement followers to the social world around them shapes not only their perception of their status within a particular society but also their life choices in relation to a belief system closely related to their political ideology. It is no accident that poor people's

movements in Latin America and religious opposition movements in general, in their choice of theological paradigms,
align with others whose goals and ideations follow parallel political attributes. And as ideological beliefs are a necessary
basis for action, "it is ideological anger, expressed through
organization and collective action, rather than discontent per
se, that tends to produce active protest" (Exum 1985, 14).
Therefore, without question, the intensity of meaning of any
one set of ideas—in this case, theological ideas—depends on
the cogency of the ideas and the potential of those who profess
them to mobilize organizational networks and resources that
can advance their goals effectively. Clearly, Catholic Action's
support of workers' issues created possibilities for a host of
Catholic workers to mobilize around several reform movements.

In Latin America many Catholic Action groups initiated
activities for university reform, rural unionizing, agrarian re-
form, and literacy programs. In addition, once Catholic Action
began to flourish in Latin America, splinter groups formed:
Juventud Obrera Catolica (JOC), the Youth Movement of
Catholic Workers; Juventud Estudiantil Catolica (JEC), the
Youth Movement of Young Catholic Students; and Juventud
Universitaria Catolica (JUC), the Youth Movement of Catholic
University Students)—all popularly based education move-
ments and popular culture movements (Gotay 1981, 50).

In Peru, the two central figures in the actual creation of
Catholic Action were Mariano Holguín of Arequipa and Pedro
Pascual Farfán of Cuzco. They were the principal architects of
a reform movement in the Church that had a twofold objective
(Klaiber 1983, 162–63). First, they established some distance
between the Church and the state, thus helping the Church
reaffirm its independence from the government. Second, they
succeeded in creating a new militant Catholicism in Peru by

giving full support to the formation of permanent lay organizations. In the 1930s the first JOC groups, modeled after similar groups in Belgium, began to spring up (Klaiber 1983, 159). Then, in 1955, the Movimiento Sindical Cristiano del Peru (MOSICP), or Christian Labor Movement of Peru, was founded. And just as it did in Italy, Belgium, Canada, France, the United States, and elsewhere, Catholic Action in Peru promoted a defense against the rising anticlerical liberalism associated with Haya de la Torre and Mariategui, the party founders of IU and APRA respectively. In essence, Catholic Action was important not only because it assisted Catholic workers during that period but also because it helped stage the transformation that characterized the Catholic Church in the 1950s and 1960s.

For many who would become supporters of liberation theology in the 1960s and 1970s, in the 1940s and 1950s there was Catholic Action. In fact, Father Gustavo Gutiérrez himself and many of the individuals around him had once been involved in Catholic Action. Moreover, many of the organizations and networks that Catholic Action created early on, particularly worker and student organizations, became useful to liberationists in the 1960s and 1970s. One of these was the National Union of Catholic Students (UNEC); two others important to the Catholic Action national network in Peru were JEC and JOC. The former enlisted high school students, and the latter focused almost exclusively on workers. These organizations nurtured friendships, effected close working relationships, and offered places where like-minded individuals could gather and mobilize around a myriad of political issues. Father Luis Fernando Crespo Tarrero (1987), director of UNEC at the Catholic University of Lima, commented: "UNEC is a community of people who question or find themselves challenged about what is going on in the country, and [who want to] explore how to establish solidarity with popular communities and organizations, or how to put one's profession at their service. It is a support movement that allows people to live their faith in line with the discoveries they go on to make in the cultural and social spheres."

According to Luis Pásara (1986), UNEC was for Catholic Action one of the three most important branches of its student movements. Established around 1941, it became influential among university students, particularly at the Catholic University of Lima, where Father Gutiérrez taught and served as the national director of UNEC. As such, he was in a position to garner broad-based support for liberation theology among students not only at his own university but at other national institutions where the student movement had been highly visible.

In an interview in the summer of 1991, Father Jorge Alvarez Calderón, once very active in Catholic Action as well as the Catholic worker movement in Peru, reflected on the influences that had caused so many priests in the 1950s and 1960s to become advocates of such dramatic change in the Church:

> After the war [World War II] several important people changed by their experiences began to arrive [in Peru]. I'm thinking about a Peruvian priest who had been trained in France. . . . He had had advanced studies in theology, much more advanced than people here, but influenced young people and supported their activities. I'm thinking also about Father Gerardo Alarco [Larrabure], and someone else who had been a layperson—that is Bishop [José] Dammert [Bellido]. He had studied law in Italy and formed part of the Catholic Action movement. These people had much influence in the universities. In other words, I would say, they were precursors to the changes, because they were so influential.

Catholic Action had a profound impact on Father Alvarez Calderón himself:

When Catholic Action first began here, I was part of what was Catholic Action at the parish level. It was made up of young people. Therefore, for me it was my first concrete experience of church that included an emphasis on what it meant to be a Christian in the world. And finally it was about making a difference around us. Over those twelve [1950s to early 1960s] years, I was able to discover what then was a specialized Catholic Action. I was one of the founders of the Juventud Estudiantil Catolica [JEC]. . . . For the most part, JEC reflected what was my world. I learned there what it meant to be a Christian in the world. I have a sense that my desire to be a priest was strongly linked to that experience. I wanted to be a priest to promote the maturation of the laity. In other words, I opted for something early on that has shaped every aspect of my life.

Clearly, Catholic Action in Peru, while perhaps less visibly important than it was in Brazil or Chile, laid a foundation of support for a theology of liberation. That foundation is important to an understanding of why the Church as a whole could make a major and decisive shift away from the rich and powerful in the 1950s and 1960s to become a more pluralistic church with a pronounced pastoral stance in favor of the marginal poor (Klaiber 1983). Assessing the influence of Catholic Action on liberationists underscores a significant characteristic of the role of ideology and of the articulators of that ideology in social movements: that ideas and strategies are embedded in very specific historical milieus. Whereas Catholic Action was important to worker movements from the Great Depression until about the 1950s, liberation theology became more relevant later on because popular movements were grappling with other issues in the 1960s and 1970s. But the social activism that emerged in Catholic Action was, in a sense, the cocoon for the metamorphoses that many churches would experience in the 1960s.

One reason for the shift away from Catholic Action was

people's dissatisfaction with its anti-Communist tendencies. In other words, as socialist analysis provided a theoretical paradigm that made the analysis of poverty more understandable, the Church found it increasingly difficult to keep socialist theories away from its followers. Many of the youth movements spawned by Catholic Action sponsored innovative Church programs, but these reforms were badly timed, coming as they did during the Cold War and the beginning of the conflict in Vietnam: "Everybody was so busy devising strategies to defeat Communism that all completely overlooked the real cause of the people's misery: nearly five centuries of social and economic oppression" (Lernoux 1982, 25). And yet no one can deny the social activism established during the more militant Catholic Action years, particularly the mobilization of certain leftist thinkers who sought to fuse their political activism with their Christianity. The type of religious-political synthesis that was made by the more radical followers of Catholic Action was important to subsequent events, because "long before actual mobilization campaigns take place, indigenous structures and subcultural networks develop and generate more or less elaborated collective identities that are the seed beds in which future collective action can come to flower" (Klandermans 1988, 174). Specifically, Catholic Action created the fertile ground upon which liberation theology could plant its seeds and flower in a new generation of people who were looking to push the Church in a new direction.

The Transition to Liberation Theology

Many former advocates of Catholic Action found themselves attracted to liberation theology during the 1960s because the theology used dependency theory, world systems theory, and socialist analyses to probe the causes of Latin America's social ills. These theories explained the international structures that created and maintained first and third world socioeconomic relations, underscoring that as long as these structures were maintained by capitalist interests, the global market systems would continually drive the exploitation of the third world. Because these theories identified the root causes of dependency and showed that dependent development would mean little change in Latin America, former members of Catholic Action groups were attracted to theological models that used social science approaches to the moral questions raised by capitalism, and that is why liberation theology spread so quickly.

The transformation that eventually occurred, from a Catholic Action stance to one of liberation, demonstrates a critical component of social movement activity. The Catholic Action movement in Peru created a critical mass of like-minded individuals who developed a collective identity in their support of the rights of workers and the poor. Although Catholic Action was later dropped because of its outright rejection of socialism, the movement did provide a consciousness and organizational support for the Catholic social teachings of that era and for others still to come. That environment also created informal networks of Catholic priests and sisters, Church activists, and theologians concerned with responding to the needs of their constituencies, and their concern made it possible for them later to embrace theological models more consistent with the political demands being placed on them by their constituencies.

Father Jorge Alvarez Calderón (1991) described the formation of one of the first of such informal networks and explained how it created opportunities for the exchange of ideas:

> The thing is that my brother [Carlos] then [around 1960, after Jorge, Gustavo Gutiérrez, and others had returned from their studies abroad] shared with Gustavo and me the tasks he had

as diocesan director of Juventudes Obrera Catolica [JOC]. And around my brother's office we had gatherings with different young priests who were working then in the still emerging popular pastorate. That was an opportunity for us to explore, to exchange, and to meet, and so on.

By this time Catholic Action had served most of its purpose, and the attention of these priests was being drawn to challenges that would result in their taking more radical stands on behalf of the popular sector.

Father Alvarez Calderón was asked why, after so many years linked to Catholic Action, he and many others changed their perspective and began supporting a theology of liberation. He responded:

> In the end, Catholic Action carried a Christian message to make the world a better place. But, in a climate like ours that message took different forms. . . . I had the impression that Catholic Action groups became very much dependent on the help of priests or parish priests. It's as if Catholic Action was reduced to organizations that were auxiliary to the priest's work. And it did not sufficiently develop a vocation, proper to the laity, of being present in the world. That speaks to Catholic Action in general. Yet the so-called specialized Catholic Action groups were the source from which all the issues were raised concerning the changes that were occurring in the country. And it is from the womb of those groups that liberation theology was given birth. Above all was the Unión Nacional de Estudiantes Catolicos [UNEC], the student group of that time. But we must also include one of the first groups, the Juventud Obrera Catolica [JOC].

The shift in attitude that Father Alvarez Calderón described produced sweeping changes in the way priests, laypeople, and others began to see their mission as Christians. They were no longer satisfied with what Catholic Action had to offer, particularly because many of them were interested in

exploring socialism. But whether or not these former supporters of Catholic Action turned to the left as they became more
radicalized, one thing became clear: the Latin American
Church was about to experience a wave of dramatic change.
Many former members of Catholic Action were transformed
into reformers, and some into revolutionaries.

Another reason for radical change in the Church was that
first in the jungle region and then in the sierras of Peru, there
began an institutionalization of an ecclesial indigenism (Marzal, 1986). In the early 1900s, three active ecclesial conscripti-
ons—the Amazons, the Ucayali, and Madre de Dios—were associated with the Augustinian, Franciscan, and Dominican
orders, respectively. By 1976 there were 857 missionaries assigned to the various localities (218 priests, 61 male and 491
female religious, and 87 laypeople). Of these men and women,
99 worked with 24 indigenous groups dispersed among 22 missions. In the Andean region too there was a significant increase in Church personnel. The new missionaries in the jungle and sierras with access to extensive resources and network
support from their distinctive congregations, began publiciz-
ing the plight of the poor in these regions and reporting the
steps they were taking to meet the challenge. Unlike the missionary drive in the first centuries of colonization, the effort
of these missionaries was to put their material and human resources at the disposal of the indigenous cause (Marzal 1986).

The Catholic Church at this time progressed through
three basic orientations and goals with regard to indigenous
peoples. The first goal was to incorporate the indigenous economy into a type of metropolitan economy through various
health and education centers, but this idea often led to eth-
nocide. The second, influenced by the rise of more radical indigenous movements, was to support the efforts of indigenous
cultures to preserve their language, way of dress, organiza-

tions, art, and so on. This emphasis led, third, to the training of missionaries as anthropologists and in other vocations of the social sciences as a way of developing greater sensitivity toward indigenous cultures. This training in social science helps explain why social analysis became crucial to various versions of the theology of liberation.

By the 1960s many special institutions had been established to preserve indigenous culture, and more were to come. For example, in 1968 the Instituto de Pastoral Andina (IPA) was created in the Cuzco region, in the southern highlands of Peru, to assess the pastoral work among the Aymara- and Quechua-speaking communities. The institute also provided a meeting place for priests and pastoral agents and published the journal *Allpanchis*. Similarly, in 1973 bishops assigned to the Amazon region created the Centro Amazonico de Antropología y Aplicación Pastoral (CAAAP); as in Cuzco, they organized courses to sensitize missionaries to indigenous causes and published a journal, *Amazonía Peruana*. In general, these efforts were meant not only to preserve indigenous culture but also to report on important political developments and social conditions in the areas involved. The publications associated with the institutes were important because the distribution of information became a central means of contacting other groups and made their situation and concerns more accessible to groups in Lima, the center of political power in Peru.

Even before theologies of liberation were published, then, many institutions in the Church were already under pressure to preserve indigenous culture and values; some indigenous communities were pushing for political autonomy; and Church workers were analyzing their economic crises in terms of dependency theory. Moreover, many Christian activists were looking for a theological model that combined their religious and political objectives. It was in that theological-pastoral-political perspective that they came to celebrate the Latin American Bishops' Conference in Medellín, Colombia, in 1968, at which liberation theology made its formal debut (Marzal 1986). And by the time liberation theology appeared, many of these groups were using Marxist analysis for much of their basic critique of society.

Leftist Trends in the Development of Liberation Theology

The general militancy that characterized some of the more radical Catholic groups in the twentieth century signaled a rising shift toward concern over political and economic issues. Many Church activists who began their careers in Catholic Action had shifted, by the early 1960s, toward more radical political positions that included dialogues with Marxists. As Rolando Ames—a representative of the United Left in the Peruvian Senate from 1985 to 1990 and a close friend of Gustavo Gutiérrez—explained in a 1991 interview, they were beginning to be disillusioned by the timid political character of Catholic Action:

> In reality, I joined UNEC because I found in Gustavo Gutiérrez [its director], who at that time had only been back in the country for two years, a more profound application of the call to the Catholic Action movement. If a bit interested, I had been critical of a Catholic Action movement that I found too rooted in the Church and too routine, full of very valiant people but with little interest in outside projects. And at that moment I was already feeling very deeply the problems the country was facing. It seemed to me that the Christian faith had some place in all of that, and that is how I joined UNEC. For me the importance of UNEC lay in its experience of Christian community.

Others shared Ames's disaffection with Catholic Action policy. Many Catholics who had begun their careers as Christian social activists in Catholic Action began to push for greater change in the Church, and one of the changes they worked for was an openness toward the left.

Around the time Church officials were becoming aware that Christians had already begun to engage in regular exchanges with Marxists, Pope John XXIII was elected to office and began a series of sweeping changes in Church policy that started with convening the Second Vatican Council, which began in 1963 and was continued by Pope Paul VI until 1965. With these popes came a new liberalism in the Catholic Church that included an openness toward exchanges between Christians and Marxists. The Catholic Action period had laid the groundwork for openness toward leftist thinking, but it was the Second Vatican Council that officially recognized the changes occurring in the lives of ordinary people and their reasons for seeing socialism as a viable alternative to capitalism.

Among the many goals John XXIII had for Vatican II was that the Church should do everything possible to bring itself closer to the people. This meant, among other things, changing the celebration of masses and rituals from Latin to the day-to-day languages of the people. The new attitude was to accept and advance the individual cultures not only of Europe but of many of the third world countries that were coming to express their own cultural identities as distinct from those of their European colonizers. And though liberation theology must not be understood as an extension of European theological thought, the challenges posed by the European theological community at Vatican II did help to create an atmosphere of receptivity to the kinds of theologies, emerging both in Europe and in the third world, that involved religious and political reform.

An important symbol of that era, not associated with liberation theology but reflecting the Church's metamorphosis in the 1960s and 1970s, was the priest Ivan Illich. Illich is note-worthy particularly for his influence on missionaries trained at his institute in Mexico and the significance of his writings for Latin America. In the early 1960s, after working in the conti-nental United States and Puerto Rico, Illich moved to Cuerna-vaca, Mexico, and established the Center for Intercultural For-mation (CIF). The purpose of CIF was to train religious personnel who were on their way to do missionary work in Latin America. The practical training it offered included the study of Spanish; even more important was the acculturation of the missionaries before they left to work in their assigned communities.

The influx of people to CIF coincided with Pope John XXI-II's call on the religious communities of the United States and Europe to send 10 percent of their personnel to Latin America. Many congregations responded, and (with the excep-tion of organizations such as Maryknoll, which had its own mis-sionary training center in Ossining, New York) sent trainees to the Cuernavaca school. Here Illich was in a unique position to provide a very practical service and at the same time to share his perspectives on the Church's mission in Latin America. The publication of his thoughts on many issues had an impact beyond the training taking place at his center. Even groups such as those from Maryknoll, who did not go through the CIF experience, were influenced by his writing.

The effect of Illich's thinking on foreign missionaries was described by a Maryknoll sister, his friend Rosa Dominga Tra-passo (1988):

> It was a very devastating experience for many people, because Ivan really pulled the rug out from under their feet . . . and ques-tioned, very much so, what their motivations were and what kind of church they were going to bring to their respective work places. He was quite destructive of the churches that most of

us had come from. It was, I'm sure, for almost everyone a very traumatic experience. Furthermore, he destroyed the myth that most of us had about ourselves, our identity as North Americans, the role of the United States in Latin America, and the model of the church we came from. . . . He destroyed the myth of the North American church that we wanted to plant here [in Latin America], and he opened us to new language. To do that, we had to go through that purgation of questioning the validity of our North American identity. I think that was very painful for many people that went through Cuernavaca. I think that was one reason that people were so angry with Ivan Illich.

In a 1988 interview the Chilean sociologist Renato Poblete added that in his work as a teacher at the Cuernavaca school from 1962 to 1965, "we were preparing foreign priests and some laity, giving them a sort of "shock treatment." It was very effective. They were coming with an attitude of the North Americans to conquer the world. I used to teach them to be realistic, to think about social and economic problems" (quoted in Smith 1991, 118–19). In an eight-year period (during the 1960s) more than 1,200 foreign priests passed through Illich's center (Smith 1991).

Ivan Illich was very important just before the emergence of liberation theology because his shock treatment served to ready the ears of foreign Church people working in Latin America for the radical ideas that were being discussed in many religious and political circles. More precisely, Illich prepared an extensive group of non-Latin, U.S.-born Church personnel for the changing tide in the Church and the specific changes occurring in the Latin American Church. As Sister Rosa Dominga observed:

> I think Ivan's influence was to open up the possibility for many people who came to Latin America to be open to what was happening here—what we would call today the beginning of liberation theology—so they would not set themselves apart from it or

feel themselves adequate without having to humble themselves to listen in Spanish or having to take their spiritual direction, their missionary direction, from Latinos or from Peruvians and not just from "professional" missionary groups, like Maryknoll, who had been here a long time and felt that maybe they knew the way to do it. (1988)

Because of Illich, many of the foreign Church workers who were spreading out all over Latin America were challenged to abandon their preconceived notions about their mission; they were forced to study the economic, cultural, and political situation of Latin America and prompted to consider more carefully their role in the Latin American Church (Smith 1991, 119).

Like the Vatican II meetings of the early 1960s, Illich and others of his generation who were not Latin Americans nevertheless served the Latin American Church by being part of the transformation process that was occurring there in the years before liberation theology. In "The Seamy Side of Charity," published in the Jesuit periodical *America*, Illich (1967a) took a very negative position in regard to North American help for Latin America (Dussel 1981, 204). He followed with "Religious Imperialism in Latin America?" (issued by the CIF) and "The Vanishing Clergyman" (1967b). Illich's ideas combined with the political theologies that had emerged in Europe to produce a challenging moment for the Church. Capitalism and imperialism were being opposed for their devastating effects on the third world, and Illich was even more controversial because he attacked the Church itself as an institution that had benefited from alignment with countries that produced inequities in Latin America and elsewhere. And his criticisms raised questions about the agendas of missionaries to Latin America and the need for their presence in the region. He questioned what it was that these missionaries wanted to take to Latin America and what kind of theological perspectives they planned to apply in their missions. Though he was criticized for being too harsh, Illich, along with those engaged in Marxist-Christian dialogues in Europe, the United States, Africa, Asia, and Latin America, produced a mind-set in favor of politically infused theologies. With the teachings of the Brazilian educator Paulo Freire (1970), the new attitude was to empower the poor so that they would take charge of their own destiny, rather than have others determine their future.

This new attitude spilled over to what came to be called "base Christian communities" (*comunidades eclesiales de base,* or CEBs). Unlike parish structures, which encompass heterogeneous populations with different outlooks and lifestyles, base Christian communities are small (on average, twelve to fifteen members), tightly knit groups of people with similar incomes, jobs, education, problems, and aspirations (Lernoux 1982, 40). They formed principally out of necessity: in every Latin American country there was a decline in recruitment to the priesthood, which required greater participation of sisters and of laypeople. They began to lead their own study groups, perform religious rituals, and provide community services. The rise of CEBs implied substantial change for the Church itself as the laity assumed broader roles and responsibility, in many cases coming to define the Church in a decentralized and participatory format that bore little resemblance to the hierarchical and highly structured institution it is commonly considered to be (Bruneau 1986, 107).

By the 1970s these popular groups had absorbed Freire's idea:

> In the "organization" which results from acts of manipulation, the people—mere guided objects—are adapted to the objectives of the manipulators. In true organization, individuals are active

in the organizing process, and the objectives of the organization are not imposed by others. In the first case, the organization is a means of "massification," in the second, a means of liberation. In Brazilian political terminology, "massification" meant the process of reducing people to a manageable, unthinking agglomeration." (1970, 145)

Liberation theology flourished in many popular sectors, particularly in the CEB environment, because it was identified as a theology that not only articulated the *plight* of the poor but in principle resonated with the *empowerment* of the poor. Its modus operandi became the vision, language, and practice of a theology that rationalized the democratic character of base Christian communities. This paradigm reversed the traditional top-down model of teaching in which the one who "knows" (the teacher) imparts knowledge to one who is presumed ignorant (Freire 1970, 36). The new educational method not only shaped the organization of many CEBs in Latin America in the 1960s but also reformed the theological models out of which the clergy and other religious personnel operated. Liberation theology was birthed in that environment and typified the communal religious moral challenge that was being posed by those constituencies.

Political movements, not only in Latin America but everywhere, were pressing theologians to focus their biblical and theological interpretations on the human condition and the moral right of religious people to protest unjust conditions as part of a fundamental moral ethic that should concern religious people everywhere. Even Pope Paul VI, in the 1965 encyclical "Gaudium et Spes" (Pastoral constitution on the church in the modern world), admitted the possibilities that could emerge with legitimate revolutions. He recognized that the world economic system caused inherent injustices; consequently, he encouraged dialogue with Marxists. He recognized that Marxism and the Churches shared a concern for the marginalized of society, even if they disagreed about solutions. For the first time, the Church boldly pursued the problem of how to synthesize material and spiritual concerns, how to link the two.

The Vatican's tolerance for and openness to Marxist-Christian exchanges at that time indirectly paved the way for theologians to make socialist critiques of capitalism an integral part of their theologies. The openness came with caution, for the pope saw some danger in the exchanges, given the avowedly atheist stance of many Marxists. But the message heard throughout the Catholic world was that the socialist critique of capitalism was going to be tolerated and that perhaps something could be learned from that critique. In Latin America this message coincided with the attraction of many political movements to some form of socialism. The success of the Cuban Revolution in 1959 became a symbol of triumph over imperialism and an initial step toward a socialist experiment.

Clearly, by the mid-1960s the Catholic Church faced the prospect that third world countries would opt for socialist governments. The greater religions of the world had to acknowledge that socialism was the form of society in one-third of the world, that it was present in Asia, Europe, and Latin America and being consciously sought in Africa (Aptheker 1970, 18). And this same political reality was shaping a new social and cultural meaning of religion, advanced in the form of revolutionary and liberation theologies. By the late 1960s, Marxist ideas had come to play a significant role in the thinking of many of the Latin American liberation theologians, thus changing the cultural meaning of religion from a stabilizing and often pacifying force to one that advocated radical political reform, including the possibility of revolution.

The political and economic reality of the 1960s in Latin

America forced many theologians to consider whether a Marxist-religious ethic was possible. At the heart of this task was the challenge of how to analyze, in a meaningful way, the root of Latin America's social problems as a consequence of capitalism and at the same time to stay close to a religious commitment. As more and more the causal link was made between capitalism and poverty, liberation theologians began seeking insight from the social sciences. Some theologians, like many social scientists, were cognizant of the impact of dependent development and the world economic system on the standard of living in Latin America and elsewhere. Much of this analysis came with the advancements of dependency and world systems theories, which looked at the social structures that created the exploitive relationship between the first and third worlds. And grassroots movements and popular insurgencies, spreading more widely and with greater urgency each day, made the task more pressing.

Although it is clear that no one liberation theologian speaks for another and that there are different strands of liberation theology, most liberationists would agree that on a fundamental level, theologies of liberation are in some way a re-call to socialism (with an emphasis on the small s). In fact, the communal spirit advocated by socialists is, as some define it, similar to the spirit behind the creation of the Christian communities of the first century. For some liberation theologians and grassroots organizers, however, the Marxist formula added another dimension: a rethinking of the religious ethical ideal as fundamentally integrated in the political system. Though the communal dimension embedded in the Marxist formula is not enough simply because it emphasizes communal rather than individual solutions, socialism does offer a political formula that can be consistent with the moral ethic professed by many liberation theologians. For this reason and others shared by socialists such as Rolando Ames, many found little contradiction between the philosophy of their political party and their attraction to the spirit of a Christian socialist principle. In fact, according to Father Gutiérrez (1973, 88):

> It was becoming more evident that the Latin American people would not emerge from their present status except by means of a profound transformation, a social revolution, which would radically and qualitatively change the conditions in which they lived. The oppressed sectors within each country were becoming aware of their class interests and of the painful road which must be followed to accomplish the breakup of the status quo.

Perhaps religions recognized that scores of millions of people in countries not yet socialist were acquiring a more or less avowedly Marxist perspective (Aptheker 1970, 18).

And where did the Latin American Catholic Church stand in the midst of all these changes? Finding the answer to this question requires an examination of another development in Church history—the radicalization of the Latin American Catholic Church itself.

The Radicalization of the Clergy

By the 1960s the popular sector had nurtured scores of revolutionary movements throughout Latin America in what has often been called the "second revolution for independence" (Gotay 1981, 36):

- a farmers' movement in the south of Peru, led by Hugo Blanco, and the rise of the FIR (Left Revolutionary Front) and other leftist groups which produced guerrilla activity in the middle of the country;
- the success of Fidel Castro's revolution and the establishment of a Marxist government in Cuba;
- popular resistance accompanying the military coup in Brazil in 1964;

- installation of a guerrilla movement in Guatemala between 1961 and 1963;
- the formation of the Frente Sandinista in the Nicaraguan pro-national liberation in 1961 and the establishment of a forceful guerrilla movement;
- the beginnings of an insurrectionist movement in Venezuela in 1962, which succeeded in uniting the leftist revolutionaries with the Communist Party;
- the new character assumed by the farmer's movement in Colombia which culminated in 1964 at Marquetalia—a socialist-influenced region on the border between the departments of Tolima and Huila—and the rise of guerrillas with an insurrectionist character;
- guerrilla uprisings in Paraguay, Chile, Argentina, Honduras, and Ecuador;
- the rise in almost every Latin American country of leftist organizations with clear insurrectionist objectives. (Gotay 1981)

According to Father Gutiérrez, "The Latin American people . . . had begun to assume their destiny . . . by organizing themselves . . . [and] becoming conscious of their situation, of the causes of their situation, organizing to defend their rights . . . as never before. . . . Latin America was taking over the reins of its destiny" (1988a).

These movements not only created dramatic changes but forced the Catholic Church to look at itself and to question its positions in many of these countries. The process of radicalization in the Peruvian Church had begun in 1955 with two political groups, in Arequipa and Lima, which converged to form the Christian Democratic Party (DC). It was organized by a group of professionals and intellectuals who began applying their Christian values to their political plan (Pásara 1986, 37).

During his political career Rolando Ames was active in the Christian Democratic Party because it was a way to link his Christianity with his political life. In 1991 the former senator commented:

> Obviously, there is an area for debate, but faith has always been at the center of my political choices. Yet I have always believed, since I was young—even when I came to discover Christian democracy, which I was active in for about two years—that I prefer not to link the Christian faith and the Christian label with a political option. That is to say, the politics that I have opted for are very much influenced by the way I have chosen to live my Christianity, but I have never thought that it is the only way to be a Christian.

For Church activists (many of whom cannot be named here because they have asked that their identities be protected), it was important that the Catholic Church openly support the popular sector, and some tested the institution's commitment to their causes by including in their protest strategy the occupation of local church buildings and cathedrals—among them the Recoleta church in Lima; the cathedral in Chiclayo, a coastal city north of Lima; the Augustinian church in Pacasmayo, another northern coastal city; and others in the southern highlands. In these moments of crisis the popular sectors began to discover that they had allies in the Church: some local priests and bishops supported them and provided sanctuary for the protesters, as one participant recounted:

> I believe it was in 1977, the military government at the time fired some 6,000 workers. The women organized themselves, and every day there were marches in the street, near the cathedral. I got involved, took beatings, . . . then some of these women took over the Recoleta church, and the priest, a good person, supported them and gave them haven. They were there for a few days.

Catalina Romero, professor of sociology at the Catholic University of Lima and, at the time of this writing, director of the Bartolomé de Las Casas Institute, described the same event in a broader sense: in the face of these events, both the secular and the priest branches of the Oficina Nacional de Información Social (ONIS), or National Office for Social Information, made declarations against the injustice to the workers (Romero 1987, 25). The priest group in ONIS, of which Father Gutiérrez was a member, was important during this radicalization period because it provided a channel for the exchange of information not only among Peruvian priests but between Peruvian and foreign priests who had been assigned to work in Peru. ONIS exchanges with lay groups and international groups such as Priests for the Third World (in Argentina) also broadened the network. Other Peruvian organizations important to this communication network included the Bartolomé de Las Casas Institute and the Centro de Estudios y Publicaciones (Center for Research and Publication), both cofounded by Gutiérrez. The laity became more active in Fe y Acción Solidaria (Faith and Actions of Solidarity), which opened avenues of communication among the base Christian communities throughout the country. Adding to the importance of these groups was the Consejo Episcopal Latinoamericano (CELAM), or Latin American Bishops' Council.

CELAM, an international organization of Latin American bishops, came into being in 1955 in Rio de Janeiro, Brazil, with the idea of paying particular attention to the interests of the Latin American Church, though not ignoring the authority of the Vatican. CELAM and other Christian groups, many of Catholic Action origin, later took positions on social issues and called for reform in the Church as well as in society. In a 1966 speech, Peru's Cardinal Juan Landázuri Ricketts declared:

I speak officially in the name of the continental hierarchy. . . . We are among those Latin Americans who are doing everything possible to understand the profound relationship between ourselves, economic structures, and politics. We are especially aware of the social revolution that is in process. We identify with it. We are trying, through our national hierarchies and the Consejo Episcopal Latinoamericano (CELAM), to spark Christian community at all levels. For the Church in Latin America, this is the hope, the struggle, the dream that is now becoming a reality: to be a servant of society in revolution—not to dominate, but to collaborate; not to make contemporary, but to inspire; not to obstruct progressive change, but to promote it. (Quoted in Romero 1987, 15)

In a lecture delivered to participants of an annual theology course, Father Gustavo Gutiérrez later added:

CELAM was important for the coordination of Latin American activities. . . . In 1963 it also raised for the president of CELAM, then a Chilean bishop, the concern of how to make the Second Vatican Council meetings more present in the Latin American Church. . . . The council meetings acted as an initial forum through which the larger Church would begin to feel the presence of the Latin American constituency. (1988b)

Gutiérrez summarized the significance of the Second Vatican Council for Latin America: its openness to the modern world, its focus on Christian unity, and the Church's concern for the poor—noting, however, that John XXIII and Paul VI had emphasized the first two themes more than the third (Gutiérrez 1985, 4).

Although the Latin American Church was only modestly represented at Vatican II, those meetings had an impact in Latin America. The Vatican's new openness gave the average person a greater role in the day-to-day functions of the Church and in liturgical rituals. And as new theological perspectives began to take into account the life of the laity, particularly lay social concerns, a new church became part of Latin America's history. Vatican II sparked hope in Latin America because the atmosphere it created in the Catholic Church opened new possibilities for the then emerging theologies of revolution and liberation. More important, organizations such as CELAM, coupled with the new openness in Rome, gave cardinals and local bishops more freedom to encourage their personnel who were working in grassroots communities to make their own decisions. Formerly, parish councils, parish priests, and other community leaders had followed a chain of command that required seals of approval by bishops and other key officials within the Church hierarchy. This liberalization not only expanded the role of the bishop in his local community but allowed the clergy and local religious communities to be more autonomous in their work and in their decisions.

There is a tendency for institutional life either to aggregate people or to disperse them. Where it aggregates them, the activities the participants engage in can create meaning for the group or mold group identity. Sometimes it can draw people together in such a way that collective action can erupt (Piven and Cloward 1977, 21). The CELAM conferences, therefore, were important for several reasons. Attended mostly by priests, Catholic and non-Catholic theologians, and bishops from various Latin American countries, they provided an opportunity for a broad exchange of ideas. In doing so, the conferences also created a national and international base for Church support of popular issues.

Many bishops began translating their religious convictions into support for the popular sector as articulated at the Medellín conference in 1968, which had sparked their "preferential option in favor of the poor"—although that phrase was not coined until the 1979 CELAM meeting, which took place in Puebla, Mexico. Other opportunities, particularly for Father

Gustavo Gutiérrez, came through the assistance of Archbishop José Dammert Bellido of Cajamarca, Peru, who not only encouraged Gutiérrez's studies but shared his theological perspective and supported other activities. Such institutional opportunities are key ingredients for an understanding of the relationships among ideology, social movements, and social movement mobilization. The Church, which had traditionally aligned itself with the richest sectors of Latin America, began a new historical trajectory there in the 1960s and 1970s: it began to provide an outlet for international exchange and the institutional base on which theologians could build support for popular movements and Church activists.

This period of Church renewal allowed many such activists to redefine the Church institution by creating and supporting their own version of Christian living, especially in the communities called CEBs. Church policies in the 1960s created a more direct line of communication among priests, sisters, other religious personnel, and the laity, empowering individuals and groups that had once been seen as spectators in a Church dominated by European men. This is not to say that the line of communication produced full understanding; clearly, women have found it necessary to continue protesting the role of second-class citizens still assigned them in a patriarchal church whose attitudes are reflected by society. But one significant outcome of the new policies was that they encouraged (even if only verbally in some instances) commitments to indigenous cultural expressions and to greater participation on the part of the laity in decision-making and day-to-day control of parish activities. By the time theologians such as Father Gutiérrez began publishing their ideas, the institutional Church—at international, national, and local community levels—was ripe for the ideas expressed in the theologies of liberation.

It is important to understand that liberation theology became widespread in popularity in part because organizations such as CELAM promoted it. Movement leaders used the resources and authority of CELAM to back their agenda. It was not until conservative elements in the Church challenged the proximity of liberation theology to Marxism that the climate for liberation theology began to change and factions within CELAM organized opposition to it (Smith 1991, 83). That later shift demonstrates the dangers that exist for movements that try to work within already established institutions such as the Catholic Church: when support for a group begins to wane, that group becomes susceptible to co-optation. In the early heyday of liberation theology, however, the coalitions mobilized by leading proponents were successful because they established networks of like-minded people within an already existing organizational network.

The 1968 CELAM participants who had already declared their own solidarity with the poor arrived in Medellín

> armed with statistical surveys, theological treatises, and sociological arguments, but the bishops had already seen the proof in the poverty outside their palace windows. Vatican II, the failures of the Alliance for Progress and the reformist governments, the upsurge of military dictatorships, and the growing misery of the Latin American people all combined to open the bishops' eyes to "the design of God in the signs of the times." (Lernoux 1982, 37–38)

More important, argued Catalina Romero (1987, 14), popular protest—led for the most part by peasants and the urban student movements—served as the backdrop for a general raising of social consciousness. In this context of protest, pronouncements by the Church sector reflected the practice and conscience of official and individual members of the hierarchy and gave new meaning to religious activism. The CELAM conference at Medellín responded to plans for remodeling the Church. The goal of the priests, theologians, and Latin American bishops who participated was to reflect on their Church activities, particularly in light of statements made in John XXIII's Vatican II encyclical "Pacem in Terris," in the United Nations 1949 Declaration of Human Rights, and by the Thirteenth General Assembly (February 1968) of the National Conference of Brazilian Bishops. As Father Gutiérrez explained: "Medellín was the result of a process. It wasn't an absolute beginning, but a pull toward a very important path. It was the result of many experiences and reflections before the conference. . . . It was a moment rooted in experiences taken up by Latin America. . . . Medellín was an itinerary of a people. . . . It was a long process in which we are still immersed" (1988b).

Because the documents published by the Second Vatican Council reflected a sense of tragedy—citing a world full of misery, marginality, and injustice in Latin America (see CELAM 1968, viii)—the urgency for social change became the overwhelming theme of the conference. Father Gutiérrez and the other theologians present solidified their vision of theology in an atmosphere of bishop support. Medellín not only introduced the world to liberation theology but suggested that these were ideas received and approved by many key bishops in the Latin American Church.

The significance of that meeting was felt almost immediately. It touched off a wave of conferences and bishops' meetings as the Church in each individual country sought to reevaluate its purposes and attempted to define what the Church and its mission meant for its local communities. Participants looked for ways to align their programs with Vatican II exhortations to make the Catholic Church a "people on a pilgrimage in the world." The Latin American Church added one more dimension: a vision of liberation.

The Medellín documents clearly stated that oppressive social structures—those that abused resources and power, exploited workers, and persisted in injustices—must be eliminated. But unlike the proposals of secular movements for achieving these goals, the CELAM interpretation of Christian movements toward liberation was based on the teachings of the gospel. For example, participants left the conference with a commitment to produce social change, but no one left with any justification for killing—which clearly posed a problem for those who supported armed dissent. There is no evidence that proponents of liberation theology in Peru, for example, have ever supported Sendero Luminoso or other guerrilla insurrections. This is partly because "no liberation theologian has provided a theological rationale for killing, and to the extent death is theologized, it is in reflections on martyrdom, the willingness to give one's life to others, not to take others' lives" (Berryman 1987, 195). Support for revolutionary movements did exist in the 1960s, particularly in the person of the "guerrilla" priest Camilo Torres, but Torres was forced out of the Church because of his activities as an armed revolutionary, and his ideas were institutionally rejected.

Other groups sought activism in Priests for the Third World (Argentina) and ONIS (Peru). ONIS was established in two stages (Romero 1982, 126). The meeting that led to its formation took place in March 1968 in the town of Cieneguilla, Peru. Participants included laypeople as well as priests. They were concerned with the socioeconomic situation of the country and called for everyone to develop an awareness of the issues. Then, in July 1968, ONIS formally came into existence in Chimbote at a meeting where priests had gathered to discuss issues relating to theology and economic development. It should be noted that ONIS never built a center or established a permanent office; rather, its community of priests reflected on social issues, made official statements relating to specific issues and events, and met regularly in cities and towns throughout the country.

It was following the meeting in Chimbote that Father Gustavo Gutiérrez's ideas of the theology of liberation began to be discussed among small groups in Peru. According to one former member, a priest who asked not to be identified, ONIS

> provided a space to reflect theologically and pastorally. It had local chapters in each diocese. . . . For example, in Chimbote, a group of priests in ONIS that gathered every fifteen days included other national members and an advisory group of regional delegates. For me it was a very important moment for theological formation. . . . There is still a small but informal network of persons from that original group that continues to get together. . . . But the end of ONIS came because of ecclesial problems—when the Peruvian Church began taking another direction.

That "direction," occurring a decade later, involved a growing institutional attack on the part of conservatives in the Church against what they saw as Marxist influences in ONIS. An article that appeared in the magazine *Realidad* (1979) sharply criticized ONIS, citing Father Gutiérrez as its leader, listing all its members, and defining it as a "Marxist group that exercised pressure and power." The article charged ONIS with falsely representing Catholicism, intervening in politics, manipulating public opinion—mainly through the efforts of pro-Communists calling themselves a priest group—and introducing foreigners into Peruvian political affairs. The last accusation reflected tensions over the high number of foreign-born priests working in Peru and the support (moral and financial) that many of them were receiving from their home congregations for social programs increasingly sympathetic to liberation theology.

It should also be noted that although Gutiérrez was a full professor of theology at the Catholic University of Lima, he never taught theology to seminarians at either the Santo Toribio Seminary or the Institute for the Study of Theology (ISET) in Lima. Even though it had been difficult for traditionalists and conservatives to limit Gutiérrez's influence in the early years of liberation theology, given its increasing popularity, they were successful in limiting his access to seminarians and other Church personnel in training. When the Vatican itself censured liberation theology in the mid-1980s, those already opposed to it were able to use institutions such as ISET and Santo Toribio to attack its supporters for spreading what they called a Marxist-inspired theology. Eventually, the opposition proved successful in Peru, in fact, the last official communiqué from ONIS came in 1979 (Romero 1991). After that date the Vatican, under the leadership of Pope John Paul II, issued several official documents cautioning against the leftist strands of liberation theology, and several priests were censured and expelled for going against official Church teachings.

The dissolution of ONIS came as one in a series of events that revealed the slowly growing countermovement to liberation theology. The fact that such groups were dissolved and that liberation theology came under attack by the right in the Catholic Church underscores the important feature of the mobilization process mentioned above: protest groups that form coalitions and mobilize resources within the same institutional structure as their opposition can be susceptible to co-optation or suppression. Even groups that succeed in transforming their institutions in favor of a certain ideological stance under one set of historical circumstances may find themselves under attack when that institutional support begins to wane under a different set of circumstances.

Nonetheless, liberation theology has not yet waned or become transformed into something else, and it is clear that it still has broad support. Priests for the Third World and ONIS were important in its early days because they created an outlet for the exchange of ideas, a support group, and a collection of individuals who would frequently publish statements in support of workers and poor people's movements. The 1968 CELAM meeting at Medellín was also important because it provided an opportunity for many involved in these groups to come forward and articulate their views before the Latin American bishops. The Medellín meeting provided the space not only where the causes of underdevelopment were identified but where views on the social and economic conditions of Latin America were understood as collective sins that had to be confronted, and the confrontation incorporated in a larger moral ethic. Those early exchanges and that conference formalized the basic premise of liberation theology. A decade (1979) later the CELAM conference at Puebla, Mexico, adopted the phrase that came to be identified with the liberationist view: "a preferential option for the poor."

For Peru and for other Latin American countries, Medellín touched off a search for new theological and doctrinal language. Even the Peruvian hierarchy began what turned out to be a series of national assemblies in its effort to confront the challenges posed in the CELAM Medellín documents. In January 1969, at the Thirty-Sixth National Episcopal Assembly of Peru, the bishops produced a further set of documents that discussed four themes: "They looked at issues of Peace and Justice, Poverty in the Church, the Apostolate of the Layperson, and Education . . . citing their option for the oppressed in their country." By 1971 the Peruvian bishops had published a document on justice, and in January 1973 they published another on evangelization (Romero 1987, 22–23).

All this activity set an institutional precedent for the Church to align itself publicly with the poor. The Peruvian hierarchy, for example, supported the agrarian reform of General Juan Velasco Alvarado (military dictator 1968–75) because his programs sided with the interests of the peasants (Romero 1987, 24). The bishops made it clear that peasants should themselves be encouraged to organize and to become agents of their own destiny. Together with Cardinal Landázuri, they also supported legislation in favor of workers. In education as well there was a push for change; for example, the religious personnel of the Sophianum High School in Lima announced in December 1968 that they would educate all social classes in the name of much-needed revolution in Peru (Romero 1987, 25).

Summary

The practice of the Latin American Church prior to the Second Vatican Council had been to absorb whatever decisions were dictated by Rome. When Vatican II gave the churches more autonomy in their respective countries, it also gave them the potential for becoming culturally distinct. Clearly, the Catholic Action movement was a first step in that direction. Its evasion of any socialist critique of capitalism hindered progress toward a real synthesis between political and theological theories; nevertheless, Catholic Action did create national and international forums for institutional exchanges between fairly progressive constituencies within the Catholic Church. And eventually, Marxist-Christian exchanges—along with the contributions of many European theologians whose various versions of political theologies advance a progressive program—proved fruitful outcomes of the Vatican II meetings.

The process of transformation in the Latin American Church, exemplified by key changes in the Peruvian Church, was underscored by the trend in some Church sectors to a commitment to the poor. This trend began when some members of Catholic Action set out to interpret the encyclical "Rerum Novarum" (Leo XIII 1891) in terms of workers' rights and more generally in terms of social justice. Subsequent Church documents opened the way for the creation of ecclesial organizations that made commitments to their local communities. More important, Vatican II allowed for national situations, as in Peru, to be dealt with by local constituencies. As the national churches turned to their continental neighbors, they discovered for themselves their similarities and their power to bring about social change. Participants in the 1968 CELAM meeting at Medellín, Colombia, sought to recognize and support what was already happening at local levels. The Medellín sessions served to clarify, crystallize, and articulate Church support for the right of poor people to protest their conditions.

This chapter has outlined part of the intricate process that laid the historical foundation for the development of liberation theology. The next chapter further defines liberation theology and analyzes the diffusion process that brought about dramatic changes in the attitudes and actions of the Peruvian hierarchy. It thus lays a foundation for understanding the relationship between the mobilization of resources and the ideological themes that create mobilization opportunities.

CHAPTER THREE

Liberation Theology in Peru

Intellectuals and their ideas may not necessarily create social movements, but they do play an integral and highly visible role in social movement activities by articulating and elaborating movement goals and strategies. The history of the emergence of liberation theology may be captured in part by studying the lives of the people who brought the theology to the forefront of Church reform. Indeed, understanding the impact that liberation theology had on the Catholic Church and on Latin America necessitates looking at the individuals who were part of the transformation process. In Peru, liberation theology began with the thinking and writing of Father Gustavo Gutiérrez Merino, who was born in Lima on June 8, 1928, and ordained a priest in 1959.

Gustavo Gutiérrez: Education and Associations

Father Gutiérrez and Father Jorge Alvarez Calderón are of the same generation: they entered the seminary together, were ordained as priests together, and have always worked closely together. Recalling their period of theological training abroad during the 1950s, Father Alvarez Calderón (1991) commented:

> The years at Louvain [in Belgium] were for me the beginning of something that I have cherished. . . . Louvain was a center of learning that gave me an opportunity to become familiar with another culture and perhaps was very much personally touched by someone who was my spiritual advisor—Jacque LeClerq. He was a man who really had made a mark on the Belgian Church, precisely on the openness the Church was experiencing at that time. He was a man who also made a mark on the Spanish-speaking countries through his writings, which were read in Peru. His writings were read a bit clandestinely in Spain, because of the Franco regime. But overall, it was a group of interesting Christian communities who read LeClerq's works. . . . That was almost at the end of his life. At that time he was in his seventies. But really that experience and his teachings made an indelible mark on all of us.

Besides student companions, Gutiérrez has remarked, other Latin Americans who were important to him in those years were not necessarily theologians, but most of them shared their priesthood in common or overlapped in their interest in liberation theology. The loose or strong friendships established during their student years allowed these young men, once in Latin America, to become part of the larger support network for the liberationist perspective.

After their studies in Europe, many of them returned home and were ordained into the Catholic priesthood. And many found themselves teaching at universities and becoming involved in specialized Catholic Action groups such as JOC, JEC, MIEC (the International Movement of Catholic Educators, and UNEC, as well as being pastors of their own churches. Father Gutiérrez, for example, became the adviser and director of UNEC, as well as full professor in the Theology Department and part-time lecturer in the Humanities Department at the Pontifical Catholic University of Lima; at the same time, he served as pastor in a parish in Rimac, a poor sector of Lima, to which he attributes his inspiration to publish *A Theology of Liberation*. In Rimac he and several colleagues founded the Bartolomé de Las Casas Institute, where they and others are able to study, publish their writings, sponsor workshops, and hold regular meetings for the exchange of ideas. (The significance of the institute for liberation theology is discussed in more detail later.)

The story of how and why Father Gustavo Gutiérrez published what he did and came to play such an important role as a theologian, priest, and advocate of the poor really began with his participation in the Catholic Action movement. Long before he became a priest, Gutiérrez had participated in Catholic Action groups as a student at the National University of San Marcos in Lima. There, he has said, he discovered two things: a politically charged lay university, and the Catholic Action organizations. According to Gutiérrez, these years as a layperson and student with ties to Catholic Action contributed to his growing perspective on liberation theology: "It was something that accumulated in my life . . . including a certain experience of Peruvian politics . . . and a Christian experience of community. Understanding the Church as a layperson was important for the development of liberation theology" (1988a).

His student years at the University of San Marcos were important to his later work also because they linked him to a myriad of social activists and to other leftists. The class mixture of the student population there provided an ideal locus for ardent political debates. Of the premier academic institutions in Peru's capital city—the Catholic University of Lima, the University of Lima, the University of the Pacific, and the University of San Marcos—only San Marcos is public, and for that reason it provides the only genuine opportunity for the children of the lower classes to establish themselves and move ahead in their professions. There are other public educational facilities as well—many of them specialized universities—but the institutions that tend to produce a list of who's who in Peruvian politics are those four.

Because of its economically diverse student population, San Marcos tends to be the most politically active institution. It is often the site of political demonstrations and teachers' strikes, and it has been long noted for producing leftist politicians, intellectuals, and organizers. In recent years it has even served as a hotbed of Sendero Luminoso membership in Lima.

This is not to say that supporters of liberation theology who have had connections with the University of San Marcos sympathize with Sendero Luminoso. As previously noted, there is little evidence in Peru that Catholic groups have supported SL at all, since "no liberation theologian has provided a theological rationale for killing" (Berryman 1987, 195). Moreover, Sendero Luminoso's attacks on Church activists, sisters, priests, and Church-sponsored programs in poor sectors of the city have been a source of the Church's rejection of Sendero Luminoso. Supporters of liberation theology are more likely to be tied to the parliamentary left, which in Peru is represented by the United Left (IU).

Two of Father Gutiérrez's most deeply shared friendships are with two noted IU politicians: Rolando Ames, a former senator; and Manuel Piqueiras, a former member of the House of Representatives. The three men met through UNEC after Father Gutiérrez had become the national director. Of his ties to UNEC, Manuel Piqueiras (1991) recalled:

> I was very young. How did I come to make this commitment to the left and to socialism? It was more due to living a certain kind of Christian practice, not so much for ideological reasons. In

other words, because of a certain Christian spiritual stance, I joined a kind of current in the Church that has come to be called the church of the poor. So working there and tied to the movements la Juventud de Estudiantes Catolicos [JEC], la Unión Nacional de Estudiantes Catolicos [UNEC], and now as a member El Movimiento de Profesionales Catolicos [MIEC], all part of the big project, I began working with the people, and later, after wanting to do something much more radical, I encountered the poor. I left the university, stopped my studies, and went for two years to work in Cajamarca, where Bishop Dammert Bellido is. After I was working there for a year, I married Susana [Villarán].

Piqueiras described himself as part of the 1968 generation of students upon whom the many events that were transforming Peru at the time had a strong impact. He cited the mass migrations from rural villages to the cities and the emergence of the *barriadas* ("shanty towns" or "squatter" townships), which in Peru have been termed *pueblos jovenes* (new settlements) to avoid the negative tone that *barriadas* implies. He spoke of the emergence of unions among factory workers, and a peasant movement that organized politically in the late 1950s and made significant strides through the 1960s. And by the late 1960s, Peru was also experiencing the reformist military dictatorship of General Velasco. Piqueiras added:

The figure of Che [Guevara, the noted Argentine leftist revolutionary who fought in the Cuban Revolution and was killed in Bolivia] was a kind of metaphor. A whole generation of university students found themselves rooted in it. In my case, there was a group that came out of the Catholic University of Peru. I emerged as the first leftist student leader—that is, leftist socialist, of the revolutionary front of socialist students, of the first openly socialist movement, which in just a few years ended up directing federated centers of students. I was part of that generation, of a whole generation of people that deeply committed itself. (1991)

That was the political climate, according to Piqueiras, in which he and many other Christian activists made decisions to join leftist organizations that were tied not only to the Catholic University of Lima but to a whole host of other universities, including the University of San Marcos, the National Agrarian University, and the National University of Engineers.

To be relevant to this generation of Christian activists, liberation theology had to promote an awareness of the class struggle; the Christian message of liberation had to be tied to their political efforts. In *A Theology of Liberation* (1973) Gutiérrez regularly refers to class struggles and to critiques of capitalism, suggesting that his intellectual training and his exchanges with the left in his own country influenced his thinking on these issues. In fact, he has noted (1988a) that although his theology of liberation did not derive directly from his student years at the University of San Marcos, where he was deeply involved in the Catholic Action movement, his experiences there and what he was exposed to as a student and layperson served later as one of a series of reference points for that theology.

It was also during his years at San Marcos that Gutiérrez met Father José Dammert Bellido, who became Bishop of Cajamarca and one of Gutiérrez's main supporters. To have the support of Bishop Dammert Bellido was particularly important because the bishop's office carried the kind of institutional clout that provided organizational resources for the sponsorship of people like Gutiérrez to study abroad, and later for the advancement of the liberationist perspective. Bishops often sponsor priests by brokering assignments for them and, as in the case of Father Gustavo Gutiérrez, act as go-betweens when priests—through their work or their writings—become controversial.

Bishop Dammert Bellido (1988) revealed how his relationship with Gutiérrez evolved:

> As I've stated in a preface to Father Gustavo Gutiérrez's book, I knew him when he was a student, when he was still at the University of San Marcos, and then when he became a priest and director of the Catholic youth movement, UNEC. . . . In part, he has been a disciple of mine in some things, then we became friends. We were active in those years, 1940s, 1950s, around social issues . . . inspired by the social doctrine of the Church begun by Pope Pius XI. . . . What we had to do then was to be active in what those policies implied and have them clear in our minds. . . . Because I had known Father Gustavo Gutiérrez when he was a university student, I became one of the ones who helped him to go off and study, first to Chile, then Belgium, France, and later Rome. I have always supported Gustavo and I continue to support any priest who can get his doctorate. . . . When there is a person, priest or layperson, who shows that kind of ability and who has theological potential, I do what I can to help them pursue their studies and to help them develop.

For Father Gutiérrez, Dammert Bellido's support meant that when he was preparing for the priesthood, he was able to travel and to study abroad. His brief sojourn in Chile before going to Europe, although it had little impact on his intellectual development, served to expose him to another Latin American Church (Gutiérrez 1988a). And subsequent travel opportunities allowed him and other priests to establish a network of like-minded individuals whose theological training and experience during a specifically tumultuous economic and political period in Latin America created a generation of like-minded theologians. This feature is significant when applied to social movement mobilization. If a movement is to spread rapidly, the communications network must already exist. And not just any communications network will do: it must be composed of like-minded people whose background, experience, and location in the social structure make them receptive to the ideas of a specific new movement (Freeman 1983, 9).

The short time in Chile allowed Gutiérrez to meet other students who would later become bishops and part of a large network of supporters of liberation theology. And other early opportunities to travel from country to country allowed Gutiérrez and other emerging liberationists, intentionally or not, to sow the seed of further support. They were later able to tap into this vast network through publications, conferences, workshops, lectureships, and other institutionally sponsored events. The network would become particularly important in the 1980s, when liberation theology came under attack by the Catholic right (as detailed in the next two chapters).

The Development Years for Liberation Theology

By the late 1960s and early 1970s, liberation theologians had found publication outlets in the magazines and journals of well-established publishing houses in Argentina, Brazil, Chile, Colombia, Mexico, Peru, Puerto Rico, Venezuela, and Uruguay. Many of their books and articles were also translated and published in the United States, Italy, France, Germany, Spain, and other countries by both religious and nonreligious publishing houses. Thus, the liberation theologians' student years were vital not only for their training as theologians but also for the opportunities that came as a result of their having developed a theological model that proved ideologically congruent with what people were feeling and experiencing at the time.

The development of liberation theology would not have been possible, however, had not the theologians themselves been deeply touched by the experiences of the people they had come to write about. In the early 1960s, for example, the Peruvian Church had begun establishing parishes in the *pueblos jovenes* of Lima. Father Jorge Alvarez Calderón was among the first Peruvian diocesan priests appointed to such a parish; usually, they were assigned to foreign missionaries. As a parish priest, he recalled, "I had it in me to promote the work of the laity. I considered that sooner or later, from that beginning, would emerge a church experience that belonged to the laity" (1991). In addition to serving his *pueblo joven* parish, he began to work along with his brother Carlos and Father Gutiérrez in Juventud Obrera Cristiana (JOC), and he cofounded El Movimiento de Trabajadores Cristianos (MTC), or the Christian Workers Movement, which by 1991 had approximately 350 members. Father Jorge Alvarez Calderón epitomized the generation of priests who had experienced Catholic Action, who had studied abroad, and who had come to feel a special calling to work with the poor.

Observing the life trajectories of these priests can help us understand the potential for individuals trained in the service of the Church to become its transformers. The collective identity of a protest group can be often represented by those individuals who come to the movement with resources and whose individual histories help unravel the intricate process by which participants are diverted from traditional careers to become voices of protest against the very institutions that formed them. The Louvain and Lyon opportunities for Gutiérrez, Alvarez Calderón, and others were perhaps the most important periods for their intellectual development as theologians, but also important were their experiences as parish priests in poor communities where they were challenged to come to a liberationist perspective.

Together, the Second Vatican Council, the Medellín and Puebla CELAM conferences, and the socioeconomic conditions of Latin America pushed these priests to advocate a theological paradigm related to the ideations of Latin America's popular movements. Vatican II alone was not enough: in February 1988, at a summer theology course sponsored annually by the Catholic University of Lima, Gutiérrez explained that although the Council provided a beginning, it was his unrest with the theological models he had studied in Europe that pushed him to think as a liberation theologian. He described "an uneasiness" that he felt as a Latin American at the Second Vatican Council meetings:

> The dominant theology at Vatican II was [still] the theology I had studied in Lyon. . . . I participated in the fourth session [of Vatican II] and felt much at ease, because these were the theologies that I had studied. . . . By 1965, however, I had been back in Peru for five years, working as a pastor, and I had other concerns. The theology I had studied did not respond to my community work [as pastor]. I felt a conflict. On the one hand, the student side of me, European, was quite happy with the Council meetings, because these were the theologies that were current. They were biblical, liturgical, and had the greatest import at the time. My Latin American social concerns, however—poverty, suffering, the poor—were not present. So I left the Council meetings with a sense of what the French call, *sentiment mélange,* or mixed feelings. So on the one hand I was content, but on the other I was dissatisfied. By 1965, I had already had many discussions with Camilo Torres, regarding the option that he had taken [armed dissent]. I carried with me that dilemma, which the Council meetings left unanswered. (1988b)

As Gutiérrez points out here, ideas take on different meanings when the social circumstances around those ideas begin to change. Ideas alone, particularly if taken from one cultural setting to be applied to another, are not necessarily useful if in their original form they lack continuity with the lives of people in the new cultural-historical setting. The theological training he and others experienced in Europe did not resonate or mesh with the social reality of Latin America. The social circumstances that they were immersed in forced them to rethink the degree to which European theological models could be useful in the Latin American context.

This reexamination did not mean that what they had gained in their theological training was useless; clearly, it had allowed them to learn the craft of theological theorizing. But their theorizing became useful when they were able to synthesize their theological training with their experiences as pastors in poor parishes and their confrontations with the political turmoil of the period. It was only then that their formula for practicing theology became meaningful for the popular sector. Thus, integral to the theologians' transformation was their exposure to the popular sector and their political activism. Intellectuals become useful to social movements when they are able to apply their training to the production of ideas that voice the moral rage of an already active population. What became clear in Latin America was that these theologians had been pressed to produce more meaningful language for those already involved in protest movements.

In 1988 one Church activist, who asked not to be identified, provided insight into how people made the religious-political synthesis in Peru.

> The problems came when we began to analyze gospel teachings *donde las papas queman* [where issues burn like hot potatoes], as we say . . . in concrete events such as the 1979 national teachers' strike, where our leaders would say, . . . "we have to organize ourselves," and we followed and marched through the streets even against the *rochabuses* [tanks filled with water used by police to dispel crowds or, in some cases, to run people down]. We marched in the face of bombs and police sticks, often running like crazy to defend ourselves. It would end and I would not be afraid, I'd prepare for the next day. During the teachers' union strike we had weeks of struggle. I felt that this strengthened my faith and my commitment. We would have get-togethers, and I often liked, no matter where I was, to make the connection be-

tween my pastoral commitment and my political activity. So I'd say to my colleagues, let's say a prayer, even though I understand that some among you are atheists. Once someone asked, what party are you in? you're an activist and you pray. All I said was that a Christian had to be very concrete. You can't say you're a Christian just because you spend all your time doing parish work. . . . I feel that Gutiérrez's and the Brazilian [Father Leonardo] Boff's theology is based on a Christ that liberates, liberates from things that destroy, like selfishness, injustice, slavery, and marginality.

For this activist and many others like her, liberation theology provided a rationale for aligning her religious convictions with her political activism. During demonstrations, such people often found themselves linked to other participants because they were all making similar ideological connections. This connectedness to the social world around them suggests that it not only shapes movement followers' perception of their status within a particular society but also shapes their life choices by relating their belief system to their political ideology (Snow and Benford 1988). Their choice of theological paradigm aligned the liberationists with the goals and ideations of an already politically active popular sector, and as the informant quoted above and others asserted, it was during demonstrations and other incidents that their shared concerns showed ideological congruence.

In a 1988 interview, Father Gustavo Gutiérrez commented on the evolution of this process of ideological congruency:

The first contact with the popular sector on the part of the Church is through its faithful, but that is not enough; little by little there is greater contact with the more active political sector. . . . That was a slow process here [in Peru] but began to happen around 1965, '66, '67. There emerged a greater relationship . . . among Christian, clearly Christian, and militant people committed to popular movements [unions, neighborhood associations, etc.]. This was all before the publication of liberation theology. That is why it is false, absolutely false, to say that the first years of liberation theology were at the level of the students in its later years at the level of the popular sector. From the beginning the popular perspective was present.

Many of the people Father Gutiérrez described became radicalized during the takeover of churches or the land-squatting incidents that had become common by the early 1970s. One such incident in Pamplona (a sector of Lima) in 1971 led to the arrest of Luis Bambaren Gastelumendi, the bishop then assigned to the city's *pueblos jovenes*. In a 1988 interview, Bishop Bambaren recalled the incident, his arrest, and its results:

> I was working with *pueblo joven* parishes and with other organizations, which the people had established. . . . *Invasiones* [illegal claims to unused land] have shaped the character of migration to Lima in the last fifty years. . . . Families would usually select an area and in one night they would claim it, making that sector a new *pueblo joven.* After an invasion, I would try to make myself available to the squatters. In early May 1971, in Pamplona, a big invasion took place. Day by day families came. The minister of housing, as was customary, was called to confront the situation. He provided some assistance, such as water. He assessed other needs and the long-term extent of those needs. . . . The police, despite these initial gestures, were ordered by the Ministry of the Interior to expel the land squatters. In the early morning hours of May 5, when the clash occurred, it left one dead and many wounded, which seriously heightened social tensions. I was able to get the body of the person killed during the clash with police to his family, which was waked at the site of the invasion. . . . The following Sunday I said mass and tried to communicate a positive reconciliatory tone. The minister of the interior misinterpreted what I was doing and had me detained the following day. Because I was a bishop, the incident was highly publicized. The publicity brought a quick solution to the situation.

Eventually the events at Pamplona led to the squatters' relocation and the creation of the *pueblo joven* Villa El Salvador. Likewise, the workers' takeover of the Recoleta church, recounted earlier, proved successful because it brought media attention to the protesters. In the face of these moments of crises, both secular groups and organizations of priests such as those in ONIS often used the Church resources at their disposal to make public declarations against injustices to workers and to the poor (Romero 1987, 25).

It was only after the theologians found themselves caught up in such protests that their usefulness as theologians took on new meaning. Their theologies of liberation elaborated the kind of protest language that was useful to building coalitions among an array of like-minded individuals from various backgrounds. For this to happen, however, clearly required liberation theologians to be exposed, through their parish work, to the communities that their theologies of liberation came to represent.

The Maturity of Liberation Theology

In essence, their schooling in Europe served the Latin American theologians in three ways: it taught them the skills necessary to speak in the language of theology; it provided a context in which they could challenge one another to incorporate their theological training into a distinctly Latin American context; and it created an environment in which they could develop deep friendships that allowed them to produce an international support network on which they could rely after they returned to their own countries. But the transformation they all underwent, out of which liberation theology developed, depended on their confrontation with insurgency movements in Latin America. The crises at home, working among the poor and participating in their activities, forced them to expand their thinking and to become advocates of reform or, for a small number, even of revolutionary change. Latin American socioeconomic reality had produced "men and women who were daily confronting misery and oppression, and who were often thinking of how to rebel against it" (Kudó 1982, 84–85). Out of that historical reality emerged Church activists, sisters, priests, and theologians who found it essential to take an active role in challenging that socioeconomic reality.

The incidents in Pamplona and at the Recoleta church were only two examples of the unrest that characterized the decades of the 1960s and 1970s. In fact, by 1968, it was reported, workers in the popular sector had staged 364 strikes; that number increased to 788 in 1973 and 779 in 1975 before leveling to 440 in 1976 (Tovar 1982, 24). And for their part, liberation theologians in Peru and elsewhere were coming to understand that unconventional measures were sometimes necessary to achieve social change and to support everything that seemed to them to help the poor.

This attitude explains why, for example, the Peruvian hierarchy publicly supported the agrarian reform of a dictator. During the 1960s and 1970s agrarian reform was the banner of two successive governments: the democratically elected Fernando Belaúnde Terry government, 1963–68, and the reformist military government under General Velasco, 1968–75 (McClintock 1989, 72). Even though Velasco had not been democratically elected, and ultimately his programs failed, the Church saw his reform efforts as advancing the interests of the poor.

Father Gutiérrez helped to radicalize the Catholic Church in this period because he and others provided a moral ethic that allowed Church activists to bridge the religious and political spheres. Manuel Piqueiras and Susana Villarán of the United Left, who like many others had gone through the UNEC experience, came to exemplify the way even children of the upper classes made the political-religious fusion. As Piqueiras (1991) recalled:

> Together, as a couple, we committed our Christianity to our political perspectives. In Cajamarca I worked with peasants during the beginning of the agrarian reform period [late 1960s]. I more or less got close to the peasantry, to their organizations, basically through my pastoral work there. . . . After that we went to live in a *pueblo joven*, a *barriada*, with our little daughter. We had married there in Cajamarca. I, as well as Susana, come from the upper classes. That time in our lives was a kind of meeting with the poor, with the other.

Similar experiences and his own networking in Catholic Action organizations proved important to Gutiérrez's emergence as a prominent theologian, particularly as he assumed a leadership role in mobilizing organizational support for the popular sector. It was his social location as a liberation theologian, priest, and activist in Catholic Action organizations and his eventual involvement in establishing the Bartolomé de Las Casas Institute and the Center for Research and Publication that proved most important to the mobilization process (Peña 1994). In other words, his influence on groups such as ONIS and UNEC, the Catholic University of Lima, and the Bartolomé de Las Casas Institute and his international status as a theologian allowed him to bridge "aggregates of individuals who shared common grievances and attributional orientations, but who . . . lacked the organizational base for expressing their discontents and for acting in pursuit of their interests" (Snow et al. 1986, 467). Gutiérrez brought those groups of individuals together by creating organizational space for them to exchange ideas, disseminate information, and share resources in their common concern for the poor. Much of this bridging was effected through organizational outreach, information diffusion, and interpersonal and intergroup contacts.

The sociologist and theologian Raúl Vidales (1993), who lived with Gutiérrez for five years (1970–75), observed that ONIS, for example, was particularly important in this bridging process. The organization of priests "carried much weight. They were listened to by the left and certainly by the right, the government, and other groups of priests, particularly those of other countries including Argentina, Bolivia, Ecuador, and Colombia. . . . We [Gutiérrez, Vidales, and other members of ONIS] traveled to interact with these groups. They often invited us to help them direct some of their activities. . . . They looked to us for guidance."

It was after the 1968 Latin American Bishops' Conference that many groups, inspired by liberation theology, began to express the need for research centers focusing on the liberation theology paradigm. Vidales suggested that this occurred because bishops such as Alfonso López Trujillo of Colombia had already started mounting opposition to liberation theology on the grounds of its leftist leanings. Thus, in 1971, in Peru, the Bartolomé de Las Casas Institute was established in the Rimac sector of Lima.

The networking made possible by such centers facilitated interchanges with other intellectuals, and not just theologians but others trained in the social sciences. As Gutiérrez (1988a) explained:

> I've never been a full-time theology professor. My work is fundamentally pastoral, and with people who mainly work in that area. Many of them simultaneously teach, so, professors in the Theology Department [at the Catholic University of Lima] are persons who work here at the Bartolomé de Las Casas, and others, including friends, who get together from time to time. . . . I do theology here, but others do sociology, psychology, political science. . . . For me it's a stimulus, because I've always believed that theology, to be language about God, has to be in contact with other disciplines.

Among those who did research at the Bartolomé de Las Casas Institute was Rolando Ames, not only a former senator of Peru but also a political scientist by training. Ames (1991) recalled:

> I worked at Bartolomé de Las Casas for three years, from 1982 to 1985. I led a research group on social movements where I worked with three people. . . . What we did was try to look at how people from Christian communities and people from popular sectors viewed politics and the state. . . . I would say that I have many friendships at Bartolomé de Las Casas. But I would not say that it is the only intellectual point of reference I have. I move in social science circles, and in Peru there are many spaces for that. I myself direct a nongovernment organization, the Instituto Democracia y Socialismo [the Institute for Democracy and Socialism], where there are Christians but also non-Christians.

Among his many activities, Ames is a professor at the Catholic University of Lima, where he has been teaching since 1967.

The important point here is that Gustavo Gutiérrez was regularly exposed to the interdisciplinary challenges brought to his institute by such people as Rolando Ames. In this manner, Gutiérrez's interdisciplinary interests combined with his intimate contacts among the people to make him and his colleagues ideal resources for the popular sector. Whenever strikes, land squatting, and other protest strategies reached crisis proportions, protesters were often supported with public statements published by organizations such as the Bartolomé de Las Casas Institute, the Comisión Episcopal de Acción Social (CEAS), and Fe y Acción Solidaria (Faith and Action of Solidarity), a lay organization. The central ingredient in the mobilization of those organizational networks was the theological rationale provided by individuals such as Gustavo Gutiérrez. Many priests, sisters, and laypeople found in liberation theology a moral message that prompted and justified their support of poor people's causes, and the organizations the liberationist perspective inspired provided institutional resources important to mounting successful movements.

Organizational Networks Available to Liberation Theology

As noted earlier, the motivation to act against social grievances is often a belief that real change can come only through action. Students of social movements frequently assume that mobilization occurs because a group believes in a cause. But shared beliefs can also become the underlying cause for network development and constituency overlap. For supporters of liberation theology, institutional networks facilitated their getting together to share their thoughts, exchange strategies for institutional reform, and identify ways in which they could develop institutional resources in their efforts to produce reform.

For example, Vidales, Gutiérrez, Tokihiro Kudó, and Cecilia Tovar began the Bartolomé de Las Casas Institute by improvising with three bookshelves. According to Vidales (1993):

> Gustavo's library was turned into community property. We began with one research area, the sociology of religion, which I initially coordinated. Cecilia [Tovar] started by organizing Gutiérrez's writings, which at the time were in longhand. She would type them and then he would edit them. . . . With the addition of other laypeople, particularly the UNEC graduates, the institute was reinforced. . . . Quickly, demand for our services grew, and when later the institute was attached to the famous summer courses [sponsored by the Theology Department of the Catholic University of Lima], we grew into a "Bartolote" [big Bartolomé].

The summer courses, which began in 1971, came to be called the Jornadas de Reflexión Teologica (theological reflection workshops). These workshops, which were designed around discussions of liberation theology, produced more opportunities for exchanges among Church activists, pastoral agents, theologians, social scientists, and others curious about the subject. In 1971 only two hundred participants attended the workshops, but by the end of the 1970s attendance had increased to six times that figure, and in 1987 the number grew to 2,496. Most participants came from Latin America, but some came from North America and Europe as well. The dramatic increases in attendance underscore the point that the key ingredient for establishing and bridging social networks was the activity of such individuals as Gustavo Gutiérrez. His liberation theology provided the basis for interest in the workshops, thus bringing together populations of likeminded individuals who might otherwise never have had opportunities to network.

Gutiérrez was in the ideal position to create such opportunities. As a professor, theologian, and parish priest who worked in a poor sector of Lima, he had legitimacy in the Church, the popular sector, the academy, and political circles. These overlapping spheres proved as important to him as he was to them. Just as liberation theology functioned to mobilize a certain type of Christian political activism, the exchange of ideas and experiences in those networks also served to sharpen Gutiérrez's own articulation of liberation theology.

The exchange of theological ideas at the summer workshops depended on both a national and an international community of supporters and curious participants. But in addition to the workshops, Gutiérrez found other opportunities to share his theological views. He regularly corresponded not only with Latin American theologians but with others, not all of them in line with the Latin American version of liberation theology. "There are many meetings, and lots of opportunities to get together," Gutiérrez (1988) has said:

> James Cone [the U.S. author of *A Black Theology of Liberation*, inspired by the Black Power movement] is a great friend of mine.

We have often gotten together at Union Theological Seminary
[in New York]. . . . I think that among the liberation theologians,
I'm one of his greater friends. . . . That's one, . . . another would
be [Robert] McAfee Brown, in another line of theology, and . . .
there is David Tracy, Gregory Baum, in Canada. I can mention
[Christian] Duquoc, a European, who was a professor of mine.
. . . He just finished publishing a book on dialogue between European theology and the theology of Latin America, . . . *Liberation
and Progress,* in French. Another person very close to me, is
[Johann Baptist] Metz. And [Edward] Schillebeeckx, in France.
There are more, . . . I could mention many. I am in frequent
contact with them because I work with the journal *Concilium;*
therefore, every year I am in contact with many European theologians. In addition, I have contacts with Allan Boesak of South
Africa, who is a good friend of mine; in reality he's like a brother.
. . . [There is] [Kwesi] Dickson from Ghana, who was also at
Union Theological Seminary; I met him in Africa. And there are
others . . . like Elizabeth Schüssler-Fiorenza. . . . When I say I
have friendships, I mean I have a theological dialogue with them.

Such a list of contacts underscores the importance of the
international church structures that often facilitated meetings and conferences. The Maryknoll congregation, Riverside
Church, and Union Theological Seminary in New York, to cite
only a few examples, regularly invited Gutiérrez to give talks
and conduct short seminars. And Maryknoll has made his work
available to audiences in the United States by translating most
of his published works into English.

The Importance of Interdisciplinary and Popular Exchange

The social scientists connected with the Bartolomé de Las
Casas Institute were heavily engaged in community research
and accordingly shaped exchanges with Father Gutiérrez
around those issues. As Gutiérrez (1988) stated, the institute's interdisciplinary focus was an important challenge for
him as a theologian. By engaging in community research, the

institute provided a context in which theological discourse benefited from the social sciences. But equally important were exchanges with the people whose realities were reflected in the information published on the basis of that research.

The institute's importance in creating resources for the popular sector became clear with the 1984 publication of Gutiérrez's *We Drink from Our Own Wells,* which he based on workshop exchanges with people from that sector. As he explained in the introduction to the book:

> Unwritten testimonies and many other texts cannot be cited in this volume, but they are with me; despite the difficulties of the task I wish to be faithful to all those witnesses. Their testimonies have made it possible for me to follow what has been happening in recent years in my country and in all Latin America. It is from the experience of this following that I have sought to write the pages of this book. (1984, 4)

In short, the testimonies of the poor made it possible for Gutiérrez to make his theological writing a concrete expression of their reality. In doing so, he exemplified the way in which the theologian, acting as a bridge between protest populations, engages his or her skills as an intellectual to articulate and bring attention to their grievances.

If left to themselves, individual consciousnesses are closed to one another; they can communicate only by means of signs that express their internal states. The sociologist Emile Durkheim (1965, 262) once said that "it is by uttering the same cry, pronouncing the same word, or performing the same gesture in regard to some object that they become and feel themselves to be in unison" (1965, 262). In other words, the use of emblems or symbols and a common language—argued here as liberation theology—were central to the formation of social groups that found common ground in solidarity with poor people's movements. That is, the moral unity or solidarity among theologians, liberationist activists, and the poor was built on a common vision communicated in a common language and expressed within a community of believers who adhered to a kind of moral unity that called for political action. And though there is a visible parallel between Durkheim's application of these ideas to whole societies and our concern here with social movements, their usefulness depends upon understanding two significant processes: how certain elements of religious belief become central to religious protest movements, and how these beliefs mobilize individuals to take action.

Twenty to thirty people participated in the workshops that led to the publication of *We Drink from Our Own Wells* (Romero 1988). The workshop participants were important to the process of transforming priest-theologians from their routine roles as mere servants of the Church into voices of protest, because those participants—many of whom were activists themselves—challenged people like Gutiérrez to use their skills as theologians to articulate effectively a theological paradigm consistent with the goals and interests of their communities. According to Romero (1988): "Developing methodology in theology is not the sole property of the theologian; all Christians can reflect on their faith. Consequently, those who took part in the theology workshops, the source of the theme of *We Drink from Our Own Wells*, were people who lived the experiences, expressed them, and later discussed them in the group." Without the contribution of those workshop participants and others like them, Gutiérrez's work would have been baseless; their testimonies gave meaning to his theology. In Peru, this was how "Father Gustavo Gutiérrez became the heart and soul of many of these groups" (Vidales 1993).

This view of the intellectual offers a better understanding of the political and intellectual life that has been a vibrant part of the popular sector in Latin America. The skill of the individual theologian was important only as part of a series of events and contributions by an array of individuals who gave meaning to liberation theology. *We Drink from Our Own Wells* was a testimony to that collective project. It came together only after years of exchanges in small workshops with a mix of individuals, theologians, and non-theologians, formally educated and uneducated, who met and shared their views on an equal footing.

On a broader scale, the book provided a bridge between local communities in struggle and a supportive national and international constituency sympathetic to their causes. The breadth of movement possibilities depends precisely on links like these. Such bridging is effected primarily by organizational outreach and information diffusion through interpersonal or intergroup networks, the mass media, the telephone, and direct mail (Snow et al. 1986, 468).

Because the Bartolomé de Las Casas Institute was interdisciplinary, it nurtured the kind of interpersonal and intergroup network exchanges important to the dissemination of liberation theology. By 1988 some seven or eight sociologists, three philosophers, two theologians, four psychologists, and four communications specialists were conducting research at the institute. Many of these researchers had been members of UNEC or students at the Catholic University of Lima, or at the time of their research were professors at the university. This pattern existed also at the Center for Research and Publication (CEP), a separate organization but one with ties to Gutiérrez and the Bartolomé de Las Casas Institute. And clearly these ties help to explain why some of the networks overlapped in membership participation. As a rule, the set of individuals interacting in one's social networks—especially one's friendship networks—is relatively homogeneous and composed of people not too different from oneself (Klandermans 1988, 175).

Adelaida Alyza, a professor of theology at the Catholic University of Lima, is a clear example not only of the fact that many of those attached to these centers were familiar to one another but of the reasons they came to congregate in the same organizations. Her initial encounter with Father Gustavo Gutiérrez was at a Social Awareness Week she attended when she was still living in Piura (a coastal city near the border with Ecuador). The first Social Awareness Week had been held in Peru in 1959; it was followed by another in 1961 for which one of the principal organizers was Bishop Dammert Bellido. It was there that Alyza first met Father Gutiérrez. At the time she was already active in the Piura chapter of UNEC, which she had joined, she explained, because

> I was experiencing a restlessness, as a Christian and as a student, that didn't seem fulfilled in any of the things or groups that the parish and the diocese had to offer. They had a perspective that wasn't part of me as a student. . . . It was during that time that I and other students attended the Semana Social [Social Awareness Week], which the diocese organized. We decided to organize ourselves as a group and link ourselves more directly in pastoral work, . . . and we met to reflect on our concerns.

At the 1961 Social Awareness Week, Alyza recalled,

> Gustavo delivered a talk that was very important in introducing me to the idea of the relation between faith and history, its context and the reality of the country. . . . What influenced me most and was a novelty for me was to discover that faith could be lived not only on a personal level . . . but in a more collective dimension that involved social commitment and was tied to being a Christian. So, Gustavo was one of the persons I met in that delegation of UNEC; . . . Father [Gerardo] Alarco [Larrabure] was the other. . . . I met them first at this important conference, and then in workshops that took place later that week. (1988)

For Alyza, being part of UNEC in the early 1960s had also coincided with her studies in the field of education. She later used many of the skills she had learned as an educator in her work with the *pueblos jovenes* of Lima. But Alyza's ties to Father Gutiérrez were strengthened when she moved to the capital in order to attend the Catholic University of Lima and pursue further studies in education.

There she continued to take part in the student movement and was eventually elected president of UNEC. Though in other Church groups it is difficult for women to hold leadership positions, it was not unusual for women to be elected to office in UNEC: its bylaws require that the presidency be shared by both sexes (Romero 1991).

Around that same time Father Gutiérrez was teaching courses at the university and had become director of UNEC. For Alyza and many students like her, who were searching for a Christian ethic that spoke to the social reality of Peru, UNEC and liberation theology provided the outlet. Alyza recalled:

> The perspective of the theological reflection that Gustavo Gutiérrez presented at the university level was very important. . . . Gustavo felt responsible for nourishing a theological formation, particularly among those who were in UNEC. . . . So, undoubtedly, Gustavo was one of the persons who introduced me to a view of theology that whetted my appetite for theological reflection, . . . and that theological perspective nourished the life of the movement. I went on to discover the link between faith and history—in general terms, the history and reality of this country and . . . forming an "option for the poor." In other words, the concern of theology reflection for the poorest sectors of this society. This theological perspective helped me decide to find work in a peasant community, work which at that time was organized around specialized . . . regional pilot development programs [which were very attractive to educators]. As I developed as a professional, I looked for greater contact with the needy sectors of this country. (1988)

This example, repeated many times in the lives of others, underscores how UNEC became a means of recruiting young professionals whose social conscience was awakened by Father Gustavo Gutiérrez and who looked to the student movement to help them realize their goals as social activists.

Like Adelaida Alyza, Catalina Romero and many other professors at the Catholic University of Lima do research at the Bartolomé de Las Casas Institute in their respective fields. This pattern is key to understanding many of the overlapping roles that intellectuals and other personnel fill. Catalina Romero first came to work at the institute because of her own personal commitments and her experiences at the university, including active work in UNEC and her discovery among the social dimensions of religion the theological perspective of Father Gutiérrez. UNEC introduced her to "the practical side of living her faith," she said. "It wasn't just an individual, personal thing or call to a particular group of people, but a call to everyone and an experience shared with popular sectors." In her own work, Romero began to analyze how people lived their faith. For her, it was an exciting time to study religion and society; the Medellín Conference had already taken place, and there was a strong sense of renewal in the Church:

> I did my thesis in 1968. I felt the times were changing, and I wanted to compare what we were discovering at various levels of Church life, . . . the Vatican's new ideas, and its connection to people. The only way to study it was to do sociology. I also wanted to see the impact at the student level, whether the ideas expressed at Vatican II stayed at the level of theology or influenced a Christian way of living. I wanted to look at that experience and to see whether it was individually or collectively applied. My interests in the study of religion began in this way. I discovered in UNEC a new way of living faith. (1988)

Subsequently, when Bartolomé de Las Casas decided in 1980 to broaden its research to include the study of the sociology of religion, it offered Professor Romero the opportunity to form her own study group.

For many students, the university experience in UNEC became an introduction to linking their religious ethic to the causes of the poor. And the dual role of Father Gutiérrez as pastor and intellectual helped him to see that students' Christianity was invariably linked to the clamors of the popular sectors. Liberation theology provided a salient model for a generation of Christian activists who came to support the liberationist perspective because they wanted to be part of something that resonated with poor people's movements, which were already making a mark on Peruvian society. UNEC and the language of liberationism opened new possibilities for religious students who were looking for some theological justification for their political activities. Father Gutiérrez provided a theological model that questioned their Christian ethic if it lacked commitment to Peru's poor. He challenged university students who were experiencing an uneasiness about how to deal with their nation's problems. Many of these students, already eager to become involved, found in UNEC and liberation theology the kind of social vision that prompted them to action.

Clearly, Father Gutiérrez's link to the Catholic University of Lima and its students and professors helped to broaden the intellectual and activist dimension waiting to be tapped. His theological perspective was formulated in a language that allowed supporters of liberation theology both to embrace the issues and concerns of the poor and to act on them as part of their Christian vocation. In this manner, his skill as a theologian provided a bridge between the urgent needs of the lower classes and persons who were looking to take some action— without, as some stated, necessarily "compromising" their Christianity with an orthodox atheist Marxism.

Students, professors, and other laypersons and Church personnel had further opportunities to converge in summer and winter theology courses. And as the work in popular Christian communities solidified, the level of interaction among local pastoral agents, priests, sisters, laypeople, and professionals strengthened. The activities of the Bartolomé de Las Casas Institute became important in bridging the diverse populations that came to the workshops by often extending the exchanges that took place there.

Other Church agencies that were supportive of the liberationist perspective included the Bishop's Social Action Commission (CEAS), created by the Church to look into human rights violations. CEAS regularly hosted meetings between parish peasant groups and other Church groups concerned with their issues. In the words of one organizer (who asked that his identity be protected:

> In CEAS there are, for example, various coordinating efforts that are responsible for supporting social pastoral work at the national level. There is a coordination with peasant groups, which means church presence at the base level. . . . Here you have opportunities for discussions on peasant national economic and political problems . . . [and] a theological and pastoral forum for the exchange of experiences. . . . This is a pastoral group concerned with human dignity and human rights at the national level. CEAS is a space for people to reflect theologically and pastorally. Bartolo [the Bartolomé de Las Casas Institute] complements all this work by providing workshops that also bring together pastoral agents to discuss specific themes: for example, issues of violence, which this country is at present experiencing.

This institutional rearrangement put many Church organizations in the role of not only providing services for the poor but also voicing public outcry against human rights violations on the part of the government. Many cases between 1983 and

1987 were reported to have been perpetrated by members of the armed forces, and it was believed that persons who disappeared were in military prisons (*CEAPAZ* 1988, 46). The Bartolomé de Las Casas Institute was also instrumental in sharing this kind of information, primarily through its magazine *Páginas*, which discussed human rights violations in several regions of the country and reported the Amnesty International findings on the 1986 massacre at El Fronton, the prison in Lima where 300 prisoners under the government of then President Alan Garcia were killed (*Páginas* 1987, 35).

Though circulated primarily in Peru, the two magazines *Páginas* and *SIGNOS* (published by the CEP) regularly circulate outside the country as well. According to Romero (1988), *Páginas* has a broader international audience, *SIGNOS* a more national readership because it was never designed for international distribution. But both publications have focused on bridging the concerns of popular groups with those of other sectors. With this effort in mind, in April 1988 *SIGNOS* expanded to include a radio program. Catalina Romero commented on this expansion:

> For us, it is important to bring to the national life of the people the experience of the popular sectors—the life of the country. It is important for us to cross the religious factor with the cultural factor of Peru, where [religion] is often reduced to an ecclesial or clerical experience, . . . to have a church that is more active, with what constitutes a national identity. . . . In a new way, to give it a dynamic, creative role. In that sense, the rich experience of the popular sectors doesn't stay in their communities; . . . it gives them a national presence. Therefore, the radio program and the dissemination of information that it provides is another area we promote. It fulfills one of our objectives—not only to expand work in the popular sector but to make it public, to bring social issues to the national forum. (1988)

Other efforts at networking and disseminating information were made possible by the Center for Research and Publication, which tended to focus chiefly on the sale of books. Together, the CEP and the Bartolomé de Las Casas Institute were the major clearinghouse for the dissemination of publications in the liberationist vein. Romero (1988) added that the institute tried to provide space in its publications for an array of contributors, often soliciting and publishing articles and commentaries by bishops, other representatives of the Church hierarchy, priests, sisters, and the Church laity.

The research and exchanges that have emerged from the Bartolomé de Las Casas Institute have facilitated contact between the popular sectors and other constituencies via *Páginas, SIGNOS,* and other publications. From its inception, *Páginas* was envisioned as a periodical whose basic mission was to be a voice for liberation theology, based on the concrete reality of the Peruvian people—particularly, the poor. This mission was reflected in the kinds of articles that the journal published. Many were biblical reflections that touched on a number of social issues—including land squatting and strikes—and, more broadly, called into moral question the disparity between the rich and the poor. Through such articles the institute made it publicly clear that its resources and mission were committed to popular concerns. *Páginas* has called urban and rural, rich and poor people together to focus on Peru's social problems—yet not exclusively. A March 1976 issue, for example, exhorted Peruvians to see those problems not as struggles limited to Peru but rather, as realities shared by many Latin Americans.

Summary

The usefulness of intellectuals to protest movements depends on their general ability to synthesize constituency goals with an ideological message that has meaning to a diverse population of protesters. Religious activists throughout Latin America used the institutional Church for their purposes by describing their grievances and their ambitions in theological language. It was in this manner that liberation theology articulated the sentiments not only of a politicized religious constituency but of the popular sector already making its own political strides.

Liberation theology became a kind of galvanizing factor, because its goals were to enter into the popular sector's struggle by articulating the plight of the poor in religious language, and to make that struggle a moral as well as a political issue. Thus, liberation theologians, Church activists, and Catholic sisters and priests provided resources for the popular movements in which they found themselves engaged. And by broadening those movements to include what some may view as unlikely allies, these protest groups availed themselves of resources in a multinetwork environment. These links depended on individuals such as Father Gustavo Gutiérrez who were able to articulate effectively the common goals shared by these diverse populations of protesters and sympathizers.

The ability to generate a set of ideas compelling to more than one protest population can be a critical factor in social movements. Here, theology provided the ideological basis on which religious constituencies could justify their political activities and thus find a moral rationale for joining or supporting the larger political movements. The adaptation of religious principles to social action depended on the interpretative skills of ministers, religious activists, and theologians who were positioned to translate and articulate for their community the ideals of the group.

Father Gustavo Gutiérrez, therefore, did not lead popular movements with his theology so much as resonate with them by capturing a political sensitivity in the language of his theology. It is in this sense that intellectuals and their ideas become an important resource in the mobilization process. In a community already anxious for change, these elements couple material resources with focused ideological goals. In this manner, in addition to the social movement organizations and other material resources whose importance is emphasized by social movement theories, ideology can play a central role in linking protest constituencies.

Studying the process by which liberation theology evolved uncovers the process by which ideas and individuals become important to social movements. The gathering of bishops, theologians, and other religious leaders of the Church at conferences in various host countries was a critical institutional resource. In fact, their ability to study abroad and to publish worldwide was a credit to the extensive resources of the Catholic Church. The Church structure and the skills of its theologians were resources that popular sectors recruited to their causes when their movements engaged the Church in their struggles. Thus, clearly important links between the popular sector and the institutional Church were individuals, such as the priest-theologians who were assigned to work in poor areas where people were already engaged in protest and where the situation demanded commitment. The popular sector's link to the institutional Church, therefore, was strengthened when such individuals felt a moral call to act on the community's behalf.

The purpose of this chapter has been to illuminate not the specific validity of religion-motivated actions but the way liberationists used certain ideological symbols and language as resources in the mobilization of protest groups. Many of the students who joined UNEC, other individuals who founded and worked at the Bartolomé de Las Casas Institute and the Center for Research and Publication, and those who attended the summer workshops that centered on liberation theology came together—whether they had strong religious convictions or not—because they believed in social justice and liberation of the poor from economic and political injustice. For its part, liberation theology served as a bridge between protest populations, linking Church activists to popular movements by justifying Church support of popular protest strategies. Additionally, the institutional Church became a haven for protesters, often facilitating exchanges among the various groups.

Ideas become useful when people adapt them to the needs of their own communities. Integral to this articulation process are the individuals who take part in the popular movements of their communities by bringing to them both old ideas and ideas adapted to meet new needs. Father Gutiérrez and others built a bridge between different constituencies and networks by providing an ideological framework meaningful to a broadly based constituency.

CHAPTER FOUR

Opposition to Liberation Theology

For some, liberation theology is solidarity with the poor. For others, liberation theology is Marxist socialism. The latter is the position of the Catholic right in Latin America, which has turned its campaign against Marxist-Leninist-Maoist socialism into a campaign against liberation theology. For the Catholic right the theology of liberation is simply a theology of the politics of the left. As a result of its campaign, some Catholic priests, sisters, and lay activists who were seen supporting strikers, squatters, or government protesters or openly supporting liberation theology have been forced to resign, were demoted, or—in the case of foreign missionaries—driven out of the country. The Catholic right has been so effective in this fight that the Vatican has censored the work of some liberation theologians and issued cautions against what it has called errancies in the theology of liberation. Given the popularity of liberation theology from the late 1960s to the late 1970s, what has happened to it at the hands of the Catholic right may seem perplexing. What occurred in Latin America to bring such a turnabout?

Exploring the answer to this question requires taking into account several important historical factors. First, liberation theology came to mean different things to different people. For progressive Catholics, it opened new doors to social activism and justified the new life-style that Christian social activists adopted when they were challenged to commit, in very radical ways, to the poor of their countries. But as adherents of the Catholic right saw it—especially after the Roman Catholic Church shifted from the era of Vatican II to that of the conservative Pope John Paul II, elected in 1978—the theology of liberation had turned these Christian social activists into Marxist radicals. As evidence, they always pointed to Father Camilo Torres. To the Catholic right, these Christian social activists were not only supporting radical political activism; they were forcing the institutional Church to choose sides against government forces.

Further, the decade of the 1980s in Peru and elsewhere was a period of heightened political tension. The presence of revolutionary guerrilla groups, primarily the Sendero Luminoso in Peru, exacerbated fears about what leftist movements would mean for the Catholic Church. There was also concern that the Church was losing ground to a growing evangelical movement (discussed below). These anxieties played on the psyche of the Catholic hierarchy, particularly in Peru, Brazil, Colombia, and Central America. Consequently, as this and the next chapter show, certain retrenchment policies began to take hold in the Latin American Catholic Church in the 1980s. First, the Church began to reject the pro-democracy and self-determining stance that characterized many of the base Christian communities. Second, it began to take exception to the anticlerical, antireligious stance that tended to characterize institutions on the left. And last, the Catholic Church began to take note of the growing Latin American evangelical movement.

Together, these factors contributed to the rising influence of the Catholic right. Thus, what happened to liberationists in Peru and elsewhere was a result of what happens when opposition groups vie for power within the same institution. What is particularly telling is how groups on both sides mobilized institutional resources in order to garner support for their movements. Further, the reaction of the Catholic right to liberation theology underscores the general rule that when threatened economically or politically, power elites of any given society look to produce movements of their own. In this case, the emergence of the Sodalitium Vitae movement in Peru and Vatican's advocacy of the theology of reconciliation converged to produce a counter-movement to liberation theology and its advocates.

Countergroups must often choose from several courses of action (Oberschall 1973, 246). Will they resort to repression, or implement reforms? Will they extend recognition to protest groups and enter into negotiations, or will they be concerned primarily with the reestablishment of order and the prosecution of the opposition? In short, will they meet the challenge to their authority with a hard or a soft response—or use a mixture of both? In looking for answers to these questions where liberation theology is concerned, one must consider how the Catholic right in Latin America was able to co-opt institutional resources, reclaim Church authority, and prosecute liberationists with charges of heresy. Yet as suggested earlier, a "softer" tactic that proved particularly effective was the substitution of the theology of reconciliation for that of liberation. This manipulation of theological discourse proved successful for a number of reasons, one of which was that the countertheme of reconciliation resonated with the outlook of people tired of civil war. In other words, the mobilization of the Catholic opposition to liberation theology was successful in the 1980s partly because of historical circumstances: it occurred during a period when people were dissatisfied with insurrectional violence.

It was true, according to the sociologist-theologian, Raúl Vidales (1993), that "the 1960s and 1970s came to be called the period of radicalization of the whole continent. It wasn't just in Peru and South America; later on it included Central America and, still later, Mexico. Many of us figuratively said that Latin America was dancing to the rhythms of South America." In the 1960s, which saw the birth of liberation theology, many countries were in the midst of growing insurgency. For some, rejecting capitalism meant joining or indirectly supporting armed revolutionary movements. For those who preferred less radical approaches, it still meant supporting the left, albeit a more parliamentary left. Those who adopted this reform stance, a group that included most supporters of the theology of liberation, felt that legislation could help solve the problems and at the same time avoid the bloodshed that was inevitable in revolutions. Even though many liberationists came to respect the actions taken by Father Camilo Torres and others, most opted for less violent protest strategies.

During this period of radicalization, the writings of Marx, Lenin, Mao, and other socialists were read with great interest. Fidel Castro and Che Guevara were viewed as heroes of the Cuban Revolution because of their success in fighting U.S. political and economic imperialism in Latin America. According to Raúl Vidales, a number of religious and lay Christian activists joined liberal-to-radical Catholic groups sympathetic to the left because they saw the left as offering an array of options for bringing about solutions to Latin America's social prob-

lems. Among the more radical Catholic groups, Vidales recalled were

> the Golconda movement, heirs of the groups established by
> Camilo Torres. There were the Priests for Socialism. Another
> group, out of Ecuador, called themselves Priests for Commu-
> nism. There was ONIS in Peru. Christian groups in Bolivia also
> committed to this cause included priest groups. There was a new
> Church, which brought all these groups together—including in-
> tellectuals as well as priests—in Brazil, Chile, and a group called
> Priests for the Third World out of Argentina. There were the
> Monteros of Uruguay. . . .
>
> All these groups were committed to giving their lives for the
> liberation of their people in one form or another. This is what we
> would later call . . . the historical womb out of which liberation
> theology was birthed. It was a period where much blood was
> spilled. Many brothers and sisters gave their lives, and they
> weren't just theologians—not at all; there emerged out of that
> restlessness a whole way of thinking, of understanding, of living,
> of proclaiming, and celebrating faith. And it all came from the
> blood of these martyrs. And without doubt, the most important
> event of the period was Medellín [the CELAM conference of
> 1968]. Medellín did not turn its back on these martyrs but recog-
> nized them as important to its very being.
>
> Later on, curiously, this same Church expressed shame
> toward these martyrs. They don't want us to speak of Camilo
> [Torres]; they don't want us to speak of [my friends] Gallegos,
> Angeleli, Cano, of bishops, priests, catechists who gave their
> lives for and are the saints of Latin America. These people filled
> the map at the time. . . . They died at the prime of their lives. . . .
> They were never traitors to the message of Jesus, as some would
> have it said. They gave their lives just as Jesus did. Latin America
> has many open furrows that no one has been able to make bar-
> ren. And they were planted and brought to fruit because these
> martyrs gave their lives and shed their blood. The theology of
> liberation came into being in the midst of all this. (1993)

In other circles the liberationists who looked for less overt
confrontational measures incorporated social scientific ap-

proaches into their efforts to alleviate Latin America's social problems. The intent was to publish and disseminate information in the hope that people would mobilize and work to bring about social change through democratic processes, thus avoiding bloodshed. Much of their analysis included using dependency theory to argue that the more global problem for Latin America was the exploitation involved in its relationship with the first world. This approach led, as the previous chapter documented, to the creation of forums for exchange, debate, research, and publication of information about the root causes of poverty. More important, these exchanges led many Catholics to examine their positions on the issues, and ultimately to make the "preferential option for the poor." As discussed earlier, after the second (1968) CELAM conference in Colombia and the third (1979) in Mexico, liberation theology became the theology of the liberals *and* the radicals.

But for the Catholic right, liberation theology was merely a conspiracy by Christian Marxists, incompatible with official Catholic social teachings simply because it embraced the idea that Marxist analysis could be useful in the critique of capitalism. For both conservatives and traditionalists, liberation theology was simply an extension of the political ideations of the popular sector and the left, who justified violence as part of their effort to produce social change. In part, then, the attacks on liberation theology must not be viewed simply as an institutional struggle over ideological paradigms but rather as a struggle over the interest articulations of opposing political interest groups.

Conservative Catholics and traditionalists reject the idea that the physical and spiritual worlds are manifested in the political lives of the people, yet it may be argued that the Catholic right has never been naive about politics and theology. In fact, its proponents are always aware of the political implications of religious ideology, because they know that "all political systems receive and respond to demands from their subjects; the process of making demands on the political system is known as interest articulation, and it is done by groups and individuals, the latter often claiming to assume the representation of important groups or of the whole society (Astiz 1969, 189). The evidence for this observation lies in the fact that the Latin American Catholic Church has for centuries exercised extensive political influence over the lives of its people. In other words, no matter how hard the adherents of the Catholic right refuse to see themselves as cogs in a political system, they have certainly attacked liberation theology as if something more than discordance over theology is at stake. It is critical to understand that the fight over liberation theology in Latin America is really a clash of political interests.

The attack on liberation theology became more effective as the Catholic right was able to ride the wave of growing local and international discontent against the left in Nicaragua, El Salvador, Colombia, and of course Peru. And as the death toll began to rise in those countries because of civil wars, the Catholic right found support among a growing number of people tired of war. Thus, when Sendero Luminoso turned against the Church and Church-sponsored programs, the Catholic right turned up its campaign against everything it deemed Marxist. At that moment, it began to use misinformation about what liberation theology was and went after anyone and any program that took a liberationist stance. It became clear that the Catholic right would seize the moment to mobilize a countermovement to liberation theology in an effort to restore the Church it saw as having been lost to the liberationists in the late 1960s and 1970s. In Peru, this countermovement was clearly helped by the tense climate that surrounded the revolutionary activities of Sendero Luminoso and the tactics the Peruvian army used to combat insurgency.

Between the Guerrillas and the Government

By the middle of the 1980s, under laws governing a state of emergency, the Peruvian military took control of Ayacucho, where Sendero Luminoso had begun its revolutionary guerrilla war. As discussed earlier, SL had become without doubt the most feared guerrilla movement in Peru; indeed,

> to most analysts, Sendero Luminoso was the ugliest guerrilla movement that had ever appeared in Latin America. Savage, sectarian, and fanatical, it [was] compared to Pol Pot's Khmer Rouge rather than to the Sandinistas or the Farabundo Marti National Liberation movement [FMLN] in El Salvador. . . . Claiming to be Maoist, it has refused to work with other Marxist groups in the country, and it has assassinated officials from Marxist and social democratic parties as readily as those from conservative parties. (McClintock 1989, 61)

The statistics show that the toll of this guerrilla war was very high. Between May 1980 and December 1987, political violence took more lives in Peru than in any other Latin American nation save El Salvador, Nicaragua, and Colombia: according to official figures, 10,541 lives. And during that same period, as the violence gradually affected more people and more parts of the country, a total of 9,534 clashes was recorded: attacks and counterattacks by both Sendero insurgents and government counterinsurgents (McClintock 1989, 63). For their part, the Peruvian military contributed to the high number of casualties. About 1979–80, before Sendero really began to step up its guerrilla activities, Amnesty International's concerns with persistent human rights violations in Peru centered primarily on the periodic large-scale, short-term arrests of trade unionists, political activists, and community leaders of the *pueblos jovenes*. On occasion, thousands of Peruvians were arrested in connection with demonstrations against the deteriorating standard of living. Arrests focused on peasants and indigenous persons from rural communities who were involved primarily in land disputes, which according to the 1980 Amnesty International reports were on the increase. Then, in 1981, accounts of torture and increasing illegal searches and arrests started to come out of the department of Ayacucho.

Attacks against the Peruvian Church, attributed to Sendero Luminoso by the government and vice versa, began as early as 1981. According to the 1982 Amnesty International report, peasant education projects supported by the Catholic Church in the highland department of Puno were threatened and dynamited, and Church authorities there protested the failure of the government to investigate the attacks. On September 19, 1981, the offices of the Apostolic Administrator of Juli were partially destroyed in a bomb blast. One month later the Juli Institute of Rural Education was bombed. Bishop Alberto I. Koenigsknecht of Juli denounced the attacks and told the press, according to Amnesty International, that he had received an anonymous letter expressing disapproval of the work of the Church "in favor of the poor" (the liberationist slogan). The letter also threatened death for him and his collaborators in rural education programs.

Many suspected government forces in these actions, because the government was clearly against what they saw as leftist sympathizers in the Church. But as time went on, it was difficult to attribute such incidents to the government alone, since Sendero was also openly criticizing the Church. Even though initially SL did not go after progressive priests and the community projects they had inspired, by the mid-1980s it clearly saw them as obstacles to the revolution: "The priests who applied the principles of liberation theology were a direct recruitment threat to the rebels in that they worked with and espoused the aspirations of the very sections of society which Sendero Luminoso wanted for itself" (Strong 1992, 173). Sendero similarly threatened leaders of community-based self-help programs, feminist organizations, and the parliamentary left; it saw these groups as thwarting the eventual demise of the Peruvian government and the fulfillment of the Maoist-Leninist revolution.

In the end, Sendero's war against the government and the government's war on Sendero both took their toll on the Peruvian people. By 1984, extrajudicial executions and "disappearances," which had been alleged only rarely in Peru before January 1983, became Amnesty International's primary concern. According to its reports, peasants were caught between Sendero Luminoso and a military which, under the declaration of a state of emergency, suspended rights of habeas corpus and other constitutional guarantees. Initially, states of emergency were limited to Ayacucho, Huancavelica, and Apurimac but later came to include other departments. During a year-long (February 1986 to July 1987) declared state of emergency in the city of Lima, military curfews not only created a tense atmosphere for ordinary citizens but also produced a number of deaths.

Almost daily, people were arrested, shot, beaten, or killed without proof that they were subversives or involved in any acts against the state. For example, on March 7, 1986, a chauffeur was shot to death by a military patrol which claimed that he ignored orders to stop. Sixteen days later a street vendor was shot for allegedly not obeying an order to stop; according to his family, he had gone out to be with friends around 11:00 P.M., was later accosted by soldiers, checked for identification, and shot in the back as he turned to leave them. On July 29, 1986, three inebriated individuals, presumed to be members of the secret police (PIP), killed four civilians as they were returning home at 3:00 A.M. from a family get-together. In August a group of marines killed a forty-two-year-old building guard only twenty minutes after the start of the curfew. Similar incidents continued in 1987 (DESCO Report 1989).

According to the Center for Research and Promotion of Development (DESCO), between July 1985 and June 1988 more civilians died as a consequence of political violence than did known subversives or military personnel. Other reports confirmed that during states of emergency, which gave the military free reign over the rights of civilians, ordinary citizens were the most frequent victims of the tense atmosphere. In October 1981 only 2.2 percent of the Peruvian population lived under a state of emergency; by December 1988 the figure was 43.2 percent (DESCO Report 1989, 34, 352).

The violence attributed to Sendero and to the Peruvian military, the economic crisis of the 1980s, and the constant rumors of an imminent military coup all contributed to a politically tense climate in Peru. Sendero and government paramilitary forces, which stepped up their attacks in the late 1980s, had begun to target political activists, organized labor, community organizers, feminists, and "do-gooder" Catholics. For Sendero, such groups only helped to maintain rather than transform the political and economic system of Peru. To the government, these groups were leftist sympathizers, suspected of aiding the Senderistas. In response, members of parliament who belonged to the United Left and some members of the Church's Commission on Social Action for Peace (CEAPAZ), risking reprisals from both the government and Sendero, took a public stance by publishing reports of incidents and naming the individuals responsible wherever possible. For example, Manuel Piqueiras headed a commission looking into human rights abuses by government paramilitary forces. During the investigation, he and others received threats against themselves and their families for what they might make public. In the end, the commission's report confirmed that paramilitary forces were involved in unconstitutional activities and responsible for human rights violations.

In the midst of all of this tension, the Catholic right carried on its own campaign against the left. It targeted not only Sendero but progressive Catholic priests, sisters, and laypeople who supported liberation theology, as if liberation theology had something to do with revolutionary activity. Taking advantage of the country's preoccupation with Sendero, it presented to the public a distorted view of liberation theology, labeling it Marxist and, on the basis of the activities of the former priest Camilo Torres's group in Colombia, supportive of revolution.

Echoing its counterparts in El Salvador, Guatemala, Nicaragua, and Colombia, the Catholic right in Peru mobilized against anything within the Church that it deemed political—including liberation theology, its supporters, and the programs they inspired. It did so chiefly by advancing a counter-theology—namely, the theology of reconciliation; however, the conflict played itself out in the political as well as the religious sphere. In other words, as the stresses of leftist-inspired revolutions in Latin America began to take their toll on the general populace, the Catholic right seized the opportunity both to censure and to co-opt the liberationist movement. But opposition to liberation theology was also being fostered at the highest levels of the Catholic Church.

The Church's Opposition
With the election of Pope John Paul II in 1978, strong resistance to liberation theology and to reform in general began to take shape. The 1979 CELAM meeting at Puebla, Mexico,

provided the Catholic right with an initial impetus toward this goal, for Puebla gave John Paul II the opportunity to revise aspects of the 1968 conference at Medellín, where Gutiérrez and other liberationists had woven their theology into the CELAM program. From its inception, Puebla was different in that "many of Latin America's leading progressive bishops were not invited or elected to participate" (Smith 1991, 211).

> Unlike Medellín, where the progressives held sway, preparations for the 1979 Puebla conference were largely controlled by a conservative faction led by a triumvirate composed of Colombian Archbishop Alfonso López Trujillo, secretary general of the Latin American Episcopal Conference (CELAM); Belgian Jesuit Roger Vekemans; and the Roman Curia's Cardinal Sebastiano Baggio, president of the Pontifical Commission for Latin America and López Trujillo's power broker at the Vatican. (Lernoux, 1982, 413)

By and large, these conservatives saw liberationists as proponents of radical forces that had been unleashed at Medellín—forces of change that had brought "a period of clerical rebellion against bishops; of emerging religious movements committed to left-wing parties, such as Christians for Socialism in Chile; and of an unprecedented number of desertions by priests and nuns, either for political motives or to marry" (Lernoux 1982, 414).

For his part, John Paul II set the tone for the critics of liberation theology in his opening address at Puebla:

> How far humanity has traveled in these ten years! . . . This third conference cannot disregard that fact. So it will have to take Medellín's conclusions as its point of departure, with all the positive elements contained therein, but without disregarding the incorrect interpretations that have sometimes resulted and that call for calm discernment, opportune criticism, and clear-cut stances. (1982, 50)

In alluding to liberation theology, the pope did not withdraw support for the cardinals and bishops present at the 1968 meeting but suggested that revision of "incorrect interpretations" would find institutional support within the Church.

The pope's resolve was quickly felt: in the early 1980s Cardinal Joseph Ratzinger, head of the Vatican's Sacred Congregation for the Doctrine of Faith, used the Puebla CELAM meeting as a springboard for leading the charge against liberation theology and its "incorrect interpretations." It should be noted that while some present at Puebla were able to include in the final platform the language of the Church's continued "preferential option for the poor," at the same time others inserted a condemnation of Marxism. Although the Puebla meeting was not a complete success for the Catholic right, therefore, it did strike an initial blow at liberation theology. And the years that followed proved more decisive. In the 1980s the Catholic right slowly began going after Church programs inspired by the theology of liberation. As some have argued, whereas the CELAM meeting in Medellín had been identified as the conference of the liberation theologians, the Puebla meeting involved representatives of three mind-sets. The first group were the conservatives, who stressed hierarchical authority; the second were the liberationists, who promoted base communities and insisted that the Church take on a style in keeping with its role of service; the third and largest group might be called centrists, who were most concerned with church unity (Berryman 1987, 103–4).

In the end, the Puebla meeting supplied right-wing groups such as the Peruvian Catholic movement Sodalitium Vitae with many quotable phrases and themes. Aware that liberation theology had become popular in many base Christian communities, in the parishes of the *pueblos jovenes,* and among lay Church activists, followers of Sodalitium Vitae found ways to reformulate it as a theology of reconciliation. But more important, occurring as it did at the onset of the Catholic right's attack against liberation theology, the 1979 Puebla meeting provided the impetus to step up the pressure.

Four years after Puebla, Cardinal Joseph Ratzinger sent the Peruvian bishops a letter listing objections to Gustavo Gutiérrez's theology (Berryman 1987, 109). And in August 1984 Ratzinger published his "Instructions on Certain Aspects of the Theology of Liberation," which focused on what he and others saw as Marxist influences in the writing of at least some liberation theologians. The cardinal believed that many liberationists operated from a fundamentally Marxist base and employed a "Marxist hermeneutic" in interpreting the Bible. In fact, "the most polemical critics of liberation theology [saw] it simply as an effort to 'baptize' Marxist revolution. Other critics acknowledge[d] the Christian intentions of liberation theology, but believe[d] that its reliance on Marxist concepts and its advocacy of socialism create[d] grave risks for the faithful" (McGovern 1990, 59).

Thus, with what the Catholic right read as approval from the Vatican, a series of actions began against the liberation theologians, the programs they inspired, and progressive Catholics who adhered to their teachings. In 1985 Father Ernesto Cardenal of Nicaragua, after years of pressure to resign from public office as minister of culture, was forced to resign from the Jesuits. Also in 1985, Father Leonardo Boff of Brazil was officially censured and silenced; on July 2, 1992, he announced that he was leaving the Catholic priesthood, explaining in an official communiqué to the international press that for the previous twenty years the Vatican and the Franciscan order had "pressured me, prohibited me from teaching, speaking, or writing, and . . . punished me."

Reflecting on the similar pressures that Father Gutiérrez has endured in Peru, Manuel Piqueiras (1991) commented:

> It seems to me that inside the structure of the Catholic Church there is an authoritarian tendency, very excluding, polar, and not very democratic. Space for dialogue is a real serious problem in Peru, especially when it comes to the Peruvian Church. So what we are seeing are clashes among different groups, all mobilized against the theology of liberation in a manner that is, first of all, distorted. The theology is not Marxist-Leninist inspired. It has a very complex relation with the social sciences. But there is a personal note in the Peruvian case. Gustavo Gutiérrez is a very exceptional man, a Christian man even before being a theologian. Really, the theology comes second. It is clear that Gustavo is a valiant person and honestly does not deserve, as a Christian, the treatment that he often gets, which really is infamous, intolerant, and distorts his position. In my view, Gustavo is a giant.

Piqueiras added: "Even though I am not well informed on Church matters, I honestly feel that his mistreatment is unwarranted, authoritarian, and dogmatic. I have not had that kind of experience as a politician." In the end, whether or not any of the liberation theologians were guilty of being Marxists or socialists, the label was enough to marginalize them and to drive some of them out of the Church.

For proponents of the Catholic right, the political maneuvering that took place at the CELAM meeting at Puebla set a new tone for the 1980s, giving them, with the Vatican's blessing, an opportunity to seize a very propitious historical moment. Subsequently, Cardinal Ratzinger provided an institutional impetus for building broad-based coalitions against the liberationists. And once the theology of reconciliation began to surface, it supplied the ideological rationale for their objectives. The Catholic right began to question everything that it could link to the inspiration or influence of liberation theology. Its adherents questioned the governing structures of the base Christian communities; the day-to-day activities of parishes, certain priests, the boards of parish councils; and the support that government protesters received from those parish priests and councils when their churches were taken over by the protesters. The prevailing attitude of the Catholic right was that there was no place for political activism in the Church and that the liberationist programs were leading to a breakdown of the authority of priests and bishops.

After Puebla, Church conservatives looked for ways to mobilize institutional resources against liberation theology. For example, as the next chapter shows, by 1983 Sodalitium Vitae—supported by other conservative groups, particularly Opus Dei—had begun to challenge liberationists by recruiting influential bishops to its cause. Institutional support from the Church hierarchy provided conservatives in Peru with the leverage they needed to compete effectively for Church resources and to mobilize against the influence of liberation theology in the parishes. And even though it can be argued that these groups have commanded a relatively narrow base of support, their link to influential bishops, both locally and internationally, has provided them with enough support to be effective. The help of Cardinal López Trujillo of Colombia, for example, has made their struggle against liberation theology a forceful threat.

Cardinal López Trujillo has been credited with the effective suppression of base Christian communities and with controlling the CELAM center in Medellín, Colombia. From that office, he and the Belgian Jesuit Roger Vekemans have been able to stage major offensives against liberation theology. As early as 1971, Vekemans set up a research center in Bogotá, Colombia, and in collaboration with then Bishop López Trujillo began to publish the journal *Tierra Nueva,* whose clear purpose was not only to attack liberation theology but also to propose an alternative kind of social analysis and theology. At the same time, López Trujillo and others were openly engaged in a planned effort to take control of CELAM.

> In November 1972 these efforts were crowned with success when López Trujillo was elected secretary-general of CELAM. He lost no time in cleaning house, collapsing the several CELAM training institutes into one, which was located in Colombia where he could watch it. The CELAM agencies dealing with missions, media, liturgy, catechetics, etc., became a platform for the attack on liberation theology. (Berryman 1987, 98–99)

Thus López Trujillo was able to cultivate contacts with the Vatican and other Latin American bishops, arguing that the Church was faced with a dangerous wave of "laicism" which, if unchecked, might overrun and eventually even eliminate the hierarchy (Levine 1986, 195).

Because of the tactics of López Trujillo, Vekemans, and others and their political alignments with right-wing politicians, some have charged that this rift within the Church has had political consequences. According to the Peruvian historian Jeffrey Klaiber:

> Conservative groups in Latin America appear not to have understood, much less accepted, this call [the call on the part of liberation theologians to opt for the poor] from the Church. On the contrary, many of them identify themselves with groups on the political right and manifest almost an obsession with the infiltration of Marxism into the Church. For these groups, Marxism refers to practically any serious reform project. That is why they often indiscriminately group Marxists with leftist non-Marxists and socialist Christians under the same banner. (1988, 422–23)

Consequently, liberationists have charged that the real reason liberation theology is under attack is their support of the popular sector.

In some general sense, the confrontation between liberationists and the Catholic right reflects the tensions between those who claim to echo the cry of the poor and others who reject their protest strategies as un-Christian. But liberationists would argue that their activities have inspired the kind of social activism that the Bible teaches and that their decision-making procedures have been based on participatory democracy. Many of the self-help programs that have emerged, whether Church-sponsored or not, have had two basic aims: day-to-day survival; and the democratic participation of their members in interpersonal relations, in the struggle against authoritarianism, and in their relationship with other popular organizations (Montes 1987, 83). For Catholics who were reared in the traditional top-down model of Church authority, however, the participatory democratic style of popular organizations clearly posed a problem.

The takeover of churches and land *invasiones* as protest strategies also forced the Church into an unprecedented mediating position between protesters and the government. For progressive parish priests and bishops, liberation theology supplied the rationale for supporting such actions. But for the Catholic right, these insurgencies, the Medellín CELAM conference, and liberation theology all converged to erode traditional Church authority and social teachings. As Oscar Alzamora Revoredo, former Archbishop of Tacna, commented in 1991:

> The theology of liberation was born at a time when various Marxist-inspired social movements were emerging. Called National Liberation Fronts, they . . . were really Marxist projects, but they also pulled together constituencies that were not exactly Marxist. . . . But when liberation theology made its debut as a unilaterally determined type of liberation forgetting about the other strands, and when they wanted to liberate people from imperial-

ism, they forgot that there were other types of imperialisms. That is why one began to question those types of theologies of liberation. Other factors brought many to question the theology of liberation: the fact that liberation theology made pacts too easily with certain types of political entities; the fact that it produced division in the Church, arguing that those who agreed with them were on the side of the poor and the exploited . . . as if that meant that those opposed to [their version of] liberation theology were in favor of exploitation and the rich and . . . were defending their interests. That is a type of disqualification, apriori, of those who do not agree with you. And this is something that is difficult to accept.

Others concurred with Alzamora's assessment and added that liberation theology was an outgrowth of a politicized social activism that went unchecked, particularly in base Christian communities. And for the Catholic right, the theologian-priest had become part of a politicized vision of liberation. Not surprisingly, what followed in the 1980s was the silencing of liberal-to-radical Catholic priests, sisters, and lay-people and their expulsion from the dioceses of powerful conservative bishops.

The turn of events in this period led to a general reorganization of experimental communities and the other projects created during the liberalization of the Church in earlier years. Liberation theology, political activism, and autonomous base Christian communities became rallying points for the revisionists of the 1980s—especially base Christian communities, because the revisionists saw the political activism of the popular sector, which constituted the bulk of CEB membership, as producing political instability. The next chapter shows how, by appealing to canon law, the Catholic right was able to replace progressive priests and to reorganize parishes wherever it saw deviations from traditional Catholic teachings. Its whole effort focused on reaffirming official Church teachings and the authority of a conservative hierarchy.

In Bishop Oscar Alzamora's opinion, reorganization was necessary because many had come to despise the "magisterium of the Church": that is, the authority claimed by the Roman Catholic Church, as divinely inspired, to teach true doctrine.

> At first I was attracted to the theology of liberation, because it attempted to make theology out of the social condition of people, . . . to say something that would help them in their everyday lives. Little by little I saw the emergence of this other group who had come out with an alternative, because they were saying . . . that you had to frame theology from what people were experiencing, And what they were experiencing was a need for reconciliation. In other words, instead of setting it up in a way where people are opposed to each other, you try to bring reconciliation. Of course, this means not to silence conflict or try to cover it over but to resolve conflict without suppressing private initiatives and leaving it to a general collectivism. What we have to do is reconcile ourselves without imposing one way to do it—to overcome conflict through reconciliation. But then others began to say that now this group is against us, and then all the suspicions emerged, which have lasted until today. (1991)

The bishop's assessment clearly shows one of the Church's greatest fears: that the impact of the guerrillas would be to destabilize society and undermine the importance of the Church among the poor. And as the Catholic right saw it, liberation theology shared in that destabilization.

In a speech delivered to a bishops' conference in Venezuela in 1988, Bishop Fernando Vargas Ruiz de Somocurcio of Arequipa, Peru, summarized what the Catholic right considered wrong with liberation theology:

> There is a group of authors who are characterized by their conflictual orientation, mostly political, and who express through their principal exponents an appropriation of "Marxist analysis." For certain sectors, the Peruvian Gustavo Gutiérrez is consid-

ered as a leader in that orientation, which the Vatican, in "Libertatis Nuntius," called erroneous and bad for the faith. . . . The ideas planted in the various currents of liberation theology have not achieved sufficient diffusion . . . because those who subscribe to the erroneous options in liberation theology have impeded its desired intention. . . . And the presence of these erroneous currents force a situation in which there must continually be clarification as to what they mean exactly, including defining their terminology.

Bishop Vargas also affirmed that the Church need not follow the liberationist paradigm but rather should

direct itself to man [*sic*], to his conscience, to his heart. It knows that grave problems penetrate all levels of social structures, and that reform is urgently needed. These changes must be guided by faith, but [made] clear and essentially defined in a call to conversion. . . . Conflict should not be minimized, but neither should it be exacerbated, nor should one point to solutions in manipulating the tensions that are there by putting aside the urgency for reconciliation. . . . Reconciliation develops a continuity with correct theological reflections about liberation that will lead rather to a theology of reconciliation, which responds to the urgencies and needs of the people of God in Latin America. (1988b, 9)

Vargas ended his speech with his support for a theology of reconciliation and the Sodalitium Vitae movement.

Bishop Ignacio Maria de Orbegozzo y Goicoechea of Chiclayo, Peru, shared Bishop Vargas's skepticism. In a 1987 article opposing liberation theology, he stated:

Some movements have surfaced (liberationist is the encompassing term used) in favor of changing oppressive and unjust structures, calling for a liberating struggle—lamentably inspired by a class struggle—which, accepting the inevitable implications for politics in evangelism, has ended in politicizing itself in an option for the poor as a class . . . that had to raise political awareness in [*concientizar*] itself first, and mobilize later as part of the liberation process. (1987a, 176)

Together, Bishops Vargas and Orbegozzo represented the growing sentiment of the Catholic right at the time. And by labeling liberation theology Marxist, they delegitimized it and gave themselves an opportunity to look for alternative uses of theological language. Thus, when Pope John Paul II began making public his writings on reconciliation themes, the Catholic right was given new life.

Meanwhile, however, an additional threat to conservative Catholicism was surfacing.

The Latin American Evangelical Churches

Although liberation theology and the spread of Communism were of major concern for conservative Catholics, another issue that arose at this time was the growing number of Protestant evangelical churches. Evangelical Protestantism is distinguished by three basic beliefs: the complete reliability and final authority of the Bible; the need to be saved through a personal relationship with Jesus Christ, often experienced or expressed as being "born again"; and the importance of spreading this message of salvation to every nation and person, a duty often referred to as the "Great Commission" (Stoll 1990, 3). The combination of this message, the disaffection with Catholic traditionalism, and the fear of the revolutionary tendency that they hear in liberation theology has pushed a large number of poor people to embrace evangelical Protestantism. Moreover, this has happened despite the fact that "whereas liberation theologians identify the United States as the main reason for Latin America's backwardness, many evangelicals hail it as a model of progress, democracy, and redemption, a veritable chosen nation" (Stoll 1990, 309). Indeed, some have charged that the evangelical movement, particu-

larly in Central America, was funded by Reagan policy supporters to fight the spread of Communism.

Whatever the reasons, the growth rate of the evangelical
churches has alarmed the Catholic Church. After five hundred
years of exclusive dominion over the hearts and minds of Latin
America's people, the Church has found itself losing ground
to the Protestant churches. Just about everywhere in Latin
America, since the 1960s, these churches have experienced
growth. They have approximately doubled their proportion in
Chile, Paraguay, Venezuela, Panama, and Haiti; tripled it in
Argentina, Nicaragua, and the Dominican Republic; and almost quadrupled it in Brazil and Puerto Rico (Stoll 1990:
8–9). In the two Central American countries of El Salvador
and Costa Rica and in the Andean countries of Peru and Bolivia, the evangelical proportion during the same period is said
to have quintupled.

In Guatemala, under the direction of former president
Rios Montt (because he himself practiced the faith), evangeli-
calism has been estimated "to have increased nearly seven
times" from 1960 to 1985 (Stoll 1990, 9) and six times in
Ecuador, Colombia, and Honduras. Thus, as the Catholic
Church was counting its martyrs, Latin Americans were aban-
doning it at an accelerating rate (Stoll 1990, xiv).

Granted, the *total* Protestant percentage of the population
is still small. Yet not surprisingly, the Catholic Church sees
the rapid evangelical growth *rate* as a threat; one bishop even
warned that Latin America was turning Protestant faster than
Central Europe did in the sixteenth century (Stoll 1990, xiv),
and a number of those interviewed for this book expressed concern about the spread of what they called *las sectas* (the sects)
in Peru. And echoing what other researchers have said about
the same phenomenon in Central America, one Catholic

Church activist described the Peruvian evangelical growth as a CIA plot to undermine the left.

One may ask what bearing this phenomenon has on a discussion of liberation theology. Part of the answer lies in the fact that large numbers of poor people in Latin American, rather than turning to revolutionary movements, are opting for quieter, less obtrusive forms of protest.

> Perhaps . . . liberation contradicts how the poor usually prefer to deal with an oppressive situation: a subtle combination of deference, foot dragging, and evasion . . .
>
> However much liberation theology spoke to aspirations for a better life, the escapism of the evangelical message was more compatible with the usual posture of the poor—fatalistic acceptance of the constraints on their continuous negotiation for survival. Under such circumstances, it was easy for liberation theology to fall out of touch with the people it claimed to represent. (Stoll 1990, 313–14)

Thus, it seems that ideological dissonance with liberation theology was not simply a matter of the Catholic right's agenda. In regions such as Central and South America, where civil wars have been taking their toll on the poor, liberationists did not consider that the response among the poor would be to turn to traditionalism and conservatism of another brand. In Peru, for example, the Pentecostals' religious and sectarian fundamentalism, with its millenarian, apocalyptic concept of the world, tallied with elements of Andean culture to fulfill the psychological needs of the poorest and most alienated sectors of Peruvian society (Strong 1992, 187).

> At around the same time that the progressive wing of the Catholic Church realized how skin-deep Christianity really was in Latin America, the Protestants started to make inroads. Almost nonexistent in Peru until 1965, the active adult congregations of the churches comprising the National Evangelical Council of Peru grew to about 2.5 per cent by 1990. (Strong 1992, 185)

In some instances, as Sendero Luminoso's war began taking its toll on the Peruvian people, the Protestant groups began to feel a kinship with the progressive Catholics. The Protestants, coming into Peru's historical picture when they did, gained ground by stressing and taking a strong position against the structural violence suffered by the poor. It was also the evangelical churches that motivated people in the state of emergency zones to defy Sendero Luminoso's call for an election boycott in 1990: "They directly helped sweep to power the previously unknown Alberto Fujimori" (Strong 1992, 185, 190).

Whatever evangelical Protestantism is and whoever is responsible for backing the movement, it is making inroads among the poor of Latin America. Some suggest that perhaps it is the warring factions within the Latin American Catholic Church that are helping the evangelical movement grow. It is clear that by the 1960s, many in the Church were articulating their dissatisfaction with its inherited medieval structures. But how to modernize it became a divisive issue.

> Another divisive issue was how to respond to oppressive governments. If the Catholic Church clung to the status quo, as it often had in the past, it would continue to alienate restless members of the lower classes. But if it turned against the power structure, its old allies would accuse it of subversion. In response to such predicaments the Catholic clergy splintered in several directions, each trying to restore the Church's authority in a different way. (Stoll 1990, 27)

And if it was true that "however much liberation theology spoke to aspirations for a better life," the poor found "the escapism of the evangelical message more compatible," then it becomes clearer why liberation theology did not find favor among all poor people (Stoll 1990, 314).

Nevertheless, there were some who opted for neither liber-

ation theology, nor for a traditional Catholicism that sided
with the landed elites, nor for *las sectas,* and these left a win-
dow of opportunity open for the Catholic right. Despite the
high rates of evangelical church growth, Latin America remains a predominantly Catholic region. Given a Catholic hierarchy in fear of the Catholic attrition rate, a Catholic movement of reconciliation could not have been more propitious.
Such a movement could adopt not only the things that made
liberation theology successful but also the things that made
the evangelical movement successful. The Catholic right,
being aware of both constituencies, promotes a brand of traditional Catholic theology that attacks liberation theology and
at the same time gives poor people what they want to hear.

The irony of the situation is that the Sodalitium Vitae
movement and the theology of reconciliation are concerned
with adopting changes in the Catholic Church that will allow
the Church to maintain itself unchanged as an institution.
Toward that end, proponents of the Catholic right are arming
themselves to do battle with both liberation theology and the
Protestant churches, and their weapon is the theology of reconciliation movement.

Summary

At the heart of the Church's attack on liberation theology was
what the theology itself represented: a product of a poor people's church. Liberation theology demands a redefinition of
the roles of bishops and priests; its new-style ministries
brought a closeness to the people that the Catholic right believed would undermine the authority of and reverence for official Church teachings.

The new Catholic traditionalism that brought the theology
of reconciliation, after living in the shadow of the popularity
of liberation theology, facilitated the Catholic right's effort

to undermine liberationism. Moreover, events in the political sphere, which had given birth to liberation theology, under the different historical circumstances of the 1980s led to the emergence of movements such as Sodalitium Vitae and the promotion of the theology of reconciliation.

The theology of reconciliation provided the rationale for the censure and expulsion of the so-called "Church radicals" in the 1980s and led to a general reorganization of experimental communities and other projects that had been created during the liberalization of the Church in earlier years. Liberation theology, political activism, base Christian communities, and the threat of Protestant expansion in the region became the rallying issues for the Catholic conservative revisionists of the 1980s. Base Christian communities were particularly important targets because the popular sector—probably the most radicalized sector of the Catholic Church—constituted the bulk of their membership.

An examination of the conflicting positions of reconciliationists and liberationists is necessary to an understanding of the ideological tensions present in the Latin American Catholic Church. On one level, the debate over liberation theology has been based simply on ideological dissonance. Events have shown, however, that the tensions reflect the conflicting political and social interests of the Church's membership. Not only did community organizations modeled after base Christian communities pose a threat to the authority of the Church hierarchy, but their networks and protest movements posed a threat to the interests of the dominant classes (this argument is made clearer in the next chapter). Consequently, the Catholic right challenged liberationists by mobilizing its own institutional resources and by proposing an alternative vocabulary and set of symbols.

The theme of reconciliation, coupled with an already organized conservative constituency, provided the ideological rationale for reasserting traditional Catholicism, but restoring the supremacy of Catholic traditionalism in the region would require mobilization around a religious ideology appealing to a varied conservative constituency—professed as the theology of reconciliation.

CHAPTER FIVE

The Catholic Right in Peru

In 1973, a group calling itself "God and Country" began appearing at the Catholic University of Lima. By 1974 the group included organizations such as the Confederación Nacionalista de Juventudes (Confederacy of Nationalist Youths) and its religious sector—Sodalitium Vitae (*Marka* 1975). The founder of the Sodalitium Vitae movement, Luis Fernando Figari, a Catholic layperson, was at the time a high school teacher at the San Isidro and Santa María schools in Lima, and many of his first recruits came from those schools.

Although Figari never entered the priesthood, he adopted the vow of celibacy, and under the Church's rule for creating "third order" organizations, he formed a lay Catholic community that allows members to take vows and to be formally recognized as a religious group within the Church. Thanks to this institutional formula and under the Vatican's protection, Sodalitium Vitae has been given institutional recognition and protection as an official Catholic religious organization. And though the 1987 Peruvian Church directory (*Directorio* 1987) listed only two priests and seven laymen as its leaders, Sodalitium Vitae's institutional alignment with the Church has allowed the movement to compete with other groups within the Church for organizational resources and networks. By 1987 the organization was reported to be operating a pastoral center and two residences for men who plan to dedicate their lives to the service of Sodalitium Vitae, and it had organized three international conferences on reconciliation.

Figari's social location within the Catholic Church has allowed him to gain access to influential bishops, develop networks, and establish centers much as Father Gustavo Gutiérrez had done earlier. The organization is cloaked in secrecy, and Figari himself does not grant interviews; employing secrecy as a strategy has allowed Sodalitium Vitae to control information about its activities as a way to keep critics at bay. Nevertheless, enough information is available from spokesperson Father Jaime Baertl, interviews with bishops, and the press to demonstrate that the Church has not only facilitated Figari's ability to spread the word on reconciliation as a countertheme to liberation theology but has also allowed him to build the organizational network necessary to mobilize an effective countermovement.

Building the Sodalitium Vitae Movement

Achieving an appointment to the faculty of the Santo Toribio Seminary in Lima was probably the most important move on Figari's part for gaining access to the Catholic Church as an institution that had much to offer supporters of the Sodalitium Vitae movement. Ties with the seminary also legitimated him at the Catholic University of Lima, which not only provided him access to new recruits but allowed him to expand his influence among a broader-based Catholic elite.

Figari's infiltration at the Catholic University of Lima—the same university where Father Gustavo Gutiérrez had clout and which UNEC used as a base—raises an important question: how, if liberation theology was popular among the UNEC students, was Sodalitium Vitae able to attract a following on the campus? One student there provided some insight: "They offered an alternative to UNEC and to the aggressive manner in which UNEC students have expressed their political perspectives. Sometimes UNEC members tend to overwhelm debates." This student represented a then growing minority of students at the Catholic University of Lima who were tired of what they called "the left's imposition on their lives."

Figari's appointment to teach at Santo Toribio proved seminal to the Sodalitium Vitae movement for another reason: there he was able to catch the attention of influential Peruvian bishops, among them Fernando Vargas Ruíz de Somocurcio of Arequipa, Oscar Alzamora Revoredo of Tacna, Augusto Vargas Alzamora (general secretary of the Peruvian Episcopate), and Ricardo Durand Florez of Callao, Lima. As time passed, these bishops effectively legitimated Figari's ideas and expanded his movement: they sponsored his conferences, did everything in their power to limit the activities of adherents of liberation theology, and promoted the theology of reconciliation as more in line with Catholic social teachings.

Opposed to the liberalization that was transforming the Latin American Catholic Church in the 1960s and 1970s, Figari and others had begun mobilizing against liberation theology as early as 1973, but they became more publicly active with their promotion of the theology of reconciliation. According to Emilio Valleguona Merea (1985, 9), Bishop of Huaráz, three important events shaped the development of Figari's thinking: the Second Vatican Council meetings, the CELAM conference at Medellín, and Pope John Paul II's call for reconciliation. Bishop Vargas of Arequipa (1988a) recalled that the theology of reconciliation was first initiated by the John Paul

II's encyclical "Reconciliato et Paenitentia" (Reconciliation and penance) in which

> the Pope depicted the global reality of negativism, extortion, death, destruction, conflicts between men [sic], and concluded that what was needed was reconciliation. Here he meant a reconciliation as a return to an encounter not only with God but with ourselves, . . . setting aside differences. . . . Reconciliation is based on a premise of sacrifice and overcoming differences in order to reconstruct a new world.

Figari expanded this concept to include a number of goals. Sincerely believing in the principles of reconciliation, he saw in it an opportunity to advance traditional Catholic theological teaching and a rhetorical weapon with which to fight liberation theology. He "envisioned a liberation in harmony with the Church's traditions. . . . The theme of love and unity among believers was key for him. He saw the fundamental Christian project that Christ had proposed: the love of the disciples and ecclesial unity; not what some currents influenced by the ideology of social science proposed" (Merea 1985, 9). Given the political climate of Peru by the 1980s, it came as no surprise that he was able to find receptive audiences.

Figari was successful because he was astute in recognizing one key element: he understood that he could not completely abandon the teachings of liberation theology, because that theology had made an indelible impact on the Latin American Church. Consequently, in developing his countertheme, he found ways to incorporate concepts of liberation. He wrote, for example:

> I believe it is Jesus who introduces me to the dynamic of liberation. . . . With this sincere conviction, however, I cannot ignore that I suffer when I see the world submerged in all types of contradictions, in all types of conflicts. . . . It is clear that before the lacerated scars of poverty stands a shameful reality of extrava-

gance and waste created by a few. . . . Humanity has opted for a world created by selfishness. . . . Therefore, each of us carries a fundamental mission, . . . to bring God's "Good News," to radiate light, hope, and warmth before a dying world. We are therefore called to be agents of reconciliation. (1985, 129–35)

Few who knew his background were fooled by Figari's newly found reconciliation rhetoric. Despite his organization's attempts at maintaining secrecy, newspapers and magazines publicized his early ties with right-wing organizations. As one news magazine reported:

> Around 1967 or 1968, a Falangist group called "Escalones Juveniles Nacionalistas" [Division of Nationalist Youths] of the San Isidro School was founded. Among its founders was Luis Fernando Figari, who remains an active member. Figari, a student of law at the Catholic University—together with don Pedro Benvenutto y Murrieta [today rector of the Pacific University]—and the young Jesuit Jorge Cáceres jointly published the journal *Tradición y Acción,* a Peruvian branch of the Society in Defense of Tradition, Family, and Property. (*Marka* 1975)

In Latin America, such organizations were known for their combined defense of traditional piety with a critique of social activism (Kselman 1986, 32). Escalones Juveniles Nacionalistas and the Defense of Tradition, Family, and Property both emphasized traditional values, asceticism, and traditional Catholic teachings. For them, reconciliation came to mean defusing political activism by encouraging opposition groups to find common ground on which to resolve their differences. In other words, reconciliation meant conflict resolution through nonviolence. This emphasis on nonviolence came to have particular appeal to the Catholic right, which openly opposed political demonstrations, strikes, land squatting, or any activity that in their view had potential for violence.

To the credit of those opponents of political demonstration, however, many of them did not propose to ignore poverty. In fact, in Lima and Arequipa, for example, Sodalitium Vitae under the guidance of Bishop Durand supported construction projects in popular communities, as well as weaving and artisan centers, food kitchens, and other service groups. The problem with their activities was, as one informant put it, that "wherever religious personnel became political they were either relocated or expelled by bishops." That sentiment was supported by a number of events that occurred in 1979 and 1982.

The Systematic Attack on Liberationist Reform

In 1982 Bishops Durand and Vargas Alzamora openly attacked a group of missionaries for their political activism in the *pueblos jovenes*. The resulting expulsion of the religious group Equipos de Misión Obrera (EMO), or the Organization of Laboring Missionaries, came to exemplify the common practice of a conservative hierarchy bent on eradicating liberation theology from Peru and Latin America. EMO's activities epitomized, for the Catholic right, everything that was wrong with workers' movements: too many members had associated themselves with factory workers' disputes and, the Catholic hierarchy believed, had become protest organizers. As conservatives saw it, EMO (also known as "Calamá," after a Chilean mine where the group successfully organized the workers) and similar groups were overstepping the Church's official position on such activities.

The reasons given for EMO's expulsion included several accusations. The first came from a Populist deputy, Daniel Linares Bazán. He implicated a group of sisters and priests in Tarapoto (a city in the northern Amazon region) the instigation of an uprising that resulted in four deaths and twenty-two injuries (*El Observador* 1982a). This incident, with the arrest of the Irish Father Rafael Keyes O'Sullivan and the North American Sister Francisca Battle, heightened tensions between conservatives and liberationists in Peru. The priest and the nun were accused of instigating demonstrations and possessing political propaganda in their homes. Their arrest served to rally conservatives in the purging of radicals. Bishop Durand not only dismantled the EMO groups who were assigned to his diocese but, by refusing to renew EMO's contracts with his parish, effectively forced them out of Peru. In a public letter, the bishop explained his actions:

> The ideas of EMO were influenced by Marxism and, from what I have learned, based on the ideas of Father Juan Caminada [a worker-priest from the Netherlands who inspired EMO). I cannot say that they were inspired by the so-called theology of liberation. For my part, I thought I had allowed sufficient time for the group as an experiment. When ideas are ill guided, one cannot expect fruitful results. . . . Since we had a clear contract, which they had not adhered to, it was impossible for me to renew, and so this prompted them to leave the country. If they attacked me a bit—well, they obeyed. It is just to say that they lived sparingly, sacrificed themselves, and were dedicated to what was an ideal for them. I conclude by pointing out that the Church has defined the limitations of its members' actions in political partisanships. (*El Observador*, 1982b).

The following year, Bishop Vargas Alzamora's defense of Durand was reported in the press:

> Speaking for some in the Peruvian Episcopate, its Secretary General, Bishop Augusto Vargas Alzamora, said that it was the Church that made the Calamá group leave the country for effecting work outside the limits of the religious pastorate and considered the incident over. Though he did not know the specifics of Calamá's actions, [he said that] Bishop Durand did well in removing them from his diocese. (*El Observador* 1983a)

The expulsions proved important because they signaled the resolve of the Catholic right in these matters: to expel Christian radicals from Church-based programs. In 1979, three years before the EMO incident, Opus Dei—the other highly visible right-wing Catholic group—had been implicated in the expulsion of SUTEP (the national teachers' union) strikers from the cathedral in Chiclayo, Peru. The SUTEP chapter of Chiclayo, where the Catholic diocese is headed by an Opus Dei member, Bishop Orbegozzo, organized to take over the cathedral as part of the strikers' strategy to gain support for their cause and to commit the Church to take their side against the government. It was not far-fetched for them to think that getting the Church involved would benefit them, since such actions had had positive results in other instances where land squatters faced off against government troops. Moreover, Church groups such as ONIS had publicly supported the strikers; in fact, ONIS had issued a letter in June 1979 saying that not only SUTEP but other unions had a right to be recognized by the government as bargaining bodies.

In contrast to ONIS, Bishop Orbegozzo chose to side with government forces. As one member of the Chiclayo SUTEP chapter recalled: "It was generally understood that someone higher up, in the diocesan office, ordered the police to remove the protesters who had taken the Cathedral; no one else would have had the authority to allow the police to enter the cathedral and arrest the protesters except the bishop himself." Newspapers confirmed that the strikers considered the bishop's office responsible for the police entering the Cathedral, but at least one article condemned the notion that Bishop Orbegozzo was directly involved in the incident: "These rumors are based on the shameful acts, like the unfortunate taking of the Cathedral by a small group of SUTEP teachers and their subsequent calumnious accusations. . . . In the same document they add that some priests, on the basis of political ideologies from the extreme left, are promoting and orienting such actions." Those who signed this article in support of Orbegozzo saw in the bishop's position, as one approvingly put it, "his constant preoccupation for the radical separation between priest actions, which are doctrinal and spiritual, and the political and social actions which are patrimonies of the Christian layperson, and for being the absolute defender of justice and human dignity, but not of sectarians or of the errant Marxists" (*El Comercio* 1979b).

Other conservatives also saw in the teachers' strike an opportunity to make their opinions public. A group of Augustinians, for example, in response to a sit-in organized by some of the protesting teachers at the Augustinian church in Pacasmayo, issued a statement to the press: "We condemn SUTEP's materialist statutes as: Marxist, Marxist atheism, enemies of the Church and in general of religion and the country. . . . We vehemently condemn the takeover of the Church of Pacasmayo, and the hunger strike of 5 professors, 2 women and 3 men, who locked themselves within the confines of the Church" (*La Prensa* 1979).

Thus, by 1979, representatives of the Catholic right everywhere in Peru were supporting one another openly, whether they were members of Sodalitium Vitae, Opus Dei, or some other conservative group. Referring to the church takeover in Pacasmayo, newspaper commentator Antonio Huertas illustrated the point: "It has already been stated . . . in the opinions of Pope John Paul II . . . that Christ should not be depicted as committed to politics or implicated in class struggles" (*La Prensa* 1979b). For many, this statement summarized the feelings of the Catholic right. For those who worked in *pueblos jovenes* or in what they liked to call the progressive parishes, however, the attitude expressed by Huertas and others who shared his feelings revealed them as persons actively working to undermine poor people's movements. Rejecting the view that the Catholic right stood for peace and against politicizing the Church, one Church activist stated: "Even though the involvement of Opus Dei Bishop Orbegozzo and his followers against the SUTEP strikers was motivated, as he and others have often stated, by official Church social teachings, their actions in effect have produced political results."

The Catholic Right's Search for a New Theology

To understand the tensions between liberationists and the Catholic right, one must recognize that for Catholic conservatives, insurgency movements and the radicalization of the Church through liberation theology challenged not only the social fabric of society but also the central authority of the Church in Peru and elsewhere in Latin America. Therefore, when groups such as Sodalitium Vitae professed a counter-theme to liberation theology, the Catholic hierarchy viewed it as a welcome alternative to the concepts, goals, and strategies of the liberation movements. The hierarchy also understood that co-opting the liberation theology movement required its active participation in the process. Thus, not surprisingly, according to the magazine *Caretas* (1977), the "Church of the Right" in the 1960s and 1970s in Peru consisted of three leading Opus Dei bishops: Ignacio de Orbegozzo, Enrique Pellach, and Luis Sanchez Moreno.

By June 1976 a group of priests called the Asociación Sacerdotal de San Pedro y San Pablo had joined the conservative ranks. Its goals involved fidelity to the institutional Church and the spread of official Church teachings. More important, the group professed its opposition to the priest group in ONIS, which they characterized as misguided by "Marxist tendencies." The association, while known for its predominantly

Opus Dei position, also had more moderate conservatives among its membership, represented by Fernando Vargas Ruíz de Somocurcio, then Bishop of Huaráz, and Ricardo Durand Florez, Bishop of Callao (*Caretas* 1977, 35).

Members of Sodalitium Vitae were not as visible because at that time they had been in existence for only three years. But when they emerged as formidable opponents of liberationism, they found support in an already mobilizing conservative hierarchy. One of the bishops who sympathized with Sodalitium Vitae was Augusto Vargas Alzamora, who from 1982 to 1986 was secretary general of the Peruvian Episcopate, the second highest position in the Peruvian Church. Bishop Vargas Alzamora made no secret of his support for Sodalitium Vitae; in fact, he was a keynote speaker at the inauguration of its conference center in Monterrico, Lima, in 1988. The bishop's direct involvement provided a threefold effect: it told the local community that the group's ideas were institutionally legitimate; it gave the movement visibility; and it provided a context and network through which to advertise the group's ideas. These three elements provided the same institutional base that was available to other conservative or liberal groups. Centered in one of Lima's wealthiest sections, the Sodalitium Vitae's pastoral center came to include a conference center, a library, and a bookstore. And as Sodalitium Vitae expanded, the center also became the site of publication for two journals: *VE* (*Vida y Espiritualidad,* or Life and Spirituality) and *FE* (*Fondo Editorial,* or Editorial Fund). These were produced by the Asociación Promotora del Apostolado (APRODEA), or the Association for the Promotion of the Apostolate, which was a group of supporters who formed the financial arm of Sodalitium Vitae.

The success and the dissemination of the theology of reconciliation depended on this kind of organizational networking. APRODEA's central goal in raising money for the construction of the pastoral center in Monterrico was to create opportunities that would facilitate the recruitment process and to gain recognition for Sodalitium Vitae from the Church hierarchy. In this latter regard, the movement succeeded. For example, Father Jaime Baertl, director of the conferences on reconciliation, revealed in a 1991 interview that close ties had been established with members of the hierarchy in Colombia, El Salvador, Nicaragua, and Brazil. Those international contacts have permitted Sodalitium Vitae to join a growing coalition of conservative groups opposed to liberation. More locally important to the movement was the number of high-ranking Peruvian bishops who began to support its activities: Bishop Vargas of Arequipa, who initiated and organized the first conference on reconciliation; Bishop Oscar Alzamora Revoredo of Tacna, the site of the third international conference on reconciliation; and, as already noted, Bishop Augusto Vargas Alzamora, highest-ranking Church supporter of the movement; and Bishop Ricardo Durand Florez.

By the mid-1980s, the Sodalitium Vitae movement had the backing of Father Armando Nieto, a noted Peruvian historian and professor at the Catholic University of Lima; German Doig, a theologian; Father Jaime Baertl; four Peruvian bishops; and other bishops from neighboring countries, notably Cardinal Alfonso López Trujillo, Archbishop of Medellín, Colombia. This impressive roster not only gave the movement broad-based support but was instrumental in tapping Church resources and networks. Indeed, the dissemination of the theology of reconciliation came to depend very heavily on the members of the Catholic Church hierarchy who proposed, organized, and sponsored annual conferences on reconciliation. The list of presenters at the Sodalitium Vitae conferences sometimes read like a who's who of conservative bishops. And the appearance of the main opponent of liberation theology in Latin America, Cardinal Alfonso López Trujillo of Colombia, as a panelist at the First International Congress on Reconciliation (1985) was one example of the kind of international mobilization that Sodalitium Vitae was able to achieve.

The Broadening Appeal of Reconciliation

The attention Sodalitium Vitae was receiving by the mid-1980s came at a critical juncture in Latin American Catholic Church history, which, as explained previously, was characterized by the political crisis that accompanied the rise of Sendero Luminoso, the fall from grace of Haya de la Torre's revolutionary alliance APRA, and the economic chaos that hit all class sectors of Peru in the 1980s. The debates that ensued about how to confront Peru's problems reflected the positions of divergent political groups, each contending for its own political solutions.

At that juncture the Catholic right began to show its preferences, whether in giving the police permission to extract protesters from churches or in promoting the idea of reconciliation and peace. Conferences led by influential bishops became important elements in the Catholic right's strategy to mobilize sentiment for reconciliation and peace. The process by which key movement players became actively involved in helping a movement grow and become visible is central to any movement's success. Sodalitium Vitae owes to the active participation of bishops its success in undermining liberation theology and advancing the theology of reconciliation.

Bishop Vargas of Arequipa described the key role bishops have played in promoting the theme of reconciliation:

> First, bishops have come to understand the meaning of reconciliation, its consequences and its implications. In order for them to deliver its message and to preach it, this is part of the process.

This is important. We should be bearers of this theology, advertisers of it. Make it become part of daily life and help people to understand it and to know that it is something positive which could fulfill their spiritual and material needs. (1988a)

In the same interview, Vargas suggested that the reason invitations to attend the reconciliation conferences were being welcomed by Church officials in Latin America and North America was that so many had lost interest in liberation theology or rejected it outright: "People expressed enthusiasm for reconciliation because it opened new possibilities. We have received letters of support from bishops in South America, Spain, Italy, and from cardinals in the United States—in particular, the cardinal from Boston. . . . They see that it is an important contribution and necessary at this juncture in the Church to achieve reconciliation."

At the First International Congress on Reconciliation, seventeen speakers and panelists represented Peru. These included the Bishop of Arequipa, who hosted the conference; Father Baertl and German Doig, two of the movement's intellectual voices; Bishop Oscar Alzamora of Tacna; Bishop Alcides Mendoza from Cuzco; Bishop Orbegozzo of Chiclayo; and a well-known Opus Dei intellectual, Father Juan Luis Cipriani. Particularly notable among the international figures was López Trujillo. Most other international participants came from neighboring countries in Latin America, but Europe was represented as well by delegates from Spain, Czechoslovakia, and Italy.

The list of presenters at these international congresses on reconciliation underscores the fact that Sodalitium Vitae's visibility has depended largely on a Catholic hierarchy eager to support efforts that undermine liberation theology. The roll of panelists for the reconciliation conferences indicates no participation by grassroots or base community organizers, and the materials available for sale to the public at the Sodalitium Vitae center in Lima show that the kind of publications usually circulated by grassroots centers are not available. These facts suggest that Sodalitium Vitae depends heavily on the leadership of supportive conservative bishops to get the message of reconciliation out to the public.

The list of panelists present at the reconciliation conference in 1985, for example, displayed the extent to which the hierarchy was promoting the Sodalitium Vitae program—including the Opus Dei hierarchy, even though its followers, beyond the scope of these conferences, are not encouraged to abandon Opus Dei in favor of Sodalitium Vitae (this explains Opus Dei participation in panel presentations but not at other levels).

Moreover, the hierarchy's presence was made known at the conference by those who professed the idea of reconciliation as a concept originated by the Vatican. According to Bishop Vargas of Arequipa, the idea for the 1985 conference on reconciliation was initiated by Pope John II's announcement that he planned a trip to Peru:

> The idea grew out of a conversation that a group of us had when we were in Rome visiting with the Pope. . . . The Pope had announced that he was making a trip to Peru. We conferred and asked what could we do in Peru. . . . It was then we proposed something on reconciliation and that it would take place in Arequipa. And the idea for the congress on reconciliation was well received. . . . The presenters represented many countries in Latin America. This gave us a feeling of universality. The conclusions [of the conference] became the basis for a theology of reconciliation. I personally submitted the document to the Pope—which at the time had only been published in brief. Later the more detailed version was published. I believe that was the starting point; there have been three congresses, the others in Callao [Lima] and Tacna. . . . I feel we should have these congresses

annually. . . . In the context of reconciliation, we should pursue new challenges—undoubtedly the issue is so important. We should deepen its application. (1988a)

Bishop Oscar Alzamora added in a 1991 interview that the conferences were meant to sensitize people to ways of fusing the ideas of liberation, reconciliation, and solidarity: "Liberation demands that I respect the other as other. Reconciliation and solidarity require that I act toward the other as part of me. That is why at the Tacna conference there were those three ideas—with solidarity as the work that completes the liberation process." The goal of the Tacna conference on reconciliation was twofold: to bring together the three themes of reconciliation, liberation, and solidarity; and to bring together theologians from other countries to discuss what Oscar Alzamora and others viewed as a more holistic theology—namely, the theology of reconciliation. Not all invitations were accepted, however:

> Theologians were brought in from a number of places. Some were invited from the other side of the border [with Chile]. That is why Tacna was chosen as the site of the conference, precisely because it is a border city. . . . But it seems that there was distrust on the part of some in the Chilean Church. Chile was at the time under Pinochet, so anything that questioned the liberation thesis was considered as favoring Pinochet's dictatorship. This was something that was far from our intention. Just because we were calling for reconciliation did not mean that we accepted military dictatorships, much less a military dictatorship as violent and unscrupulous as was that of the Pinochet government. But, in the end, that distrust proved difficult to overcome, and the cooperation that we had expected from the Chilean bishops never came. (1991)

Despite the Chilean bishops' absence, the conference went on as scheduled, and others followed.

According to Bishop Vargas, many who attended the conferences on reconciliation were in search of a viable theology for their ministries.

> Many had come with that idea. Some came with great curiosity and others with a yearning to find something different. . . . What was in the air at the time was an interest in reconciliation. Unfortunately, the facility [for the Arequipa conference] was too small. We didn't anticipate the numbers; we could easily have had a thousand people. We had six hundred because others didn't fit, but really the response was overwhelming. People spoke freely; there were many opportunities for questions and interruptions—this is what really made it successful. (1988a)

And indeed, published documents from the Arequipa conference confirm that six hundred persons representing many areas of Peru, were in attendance between January 11 and January 13, 1985, at the Convent of Santa Catalina in Arequipa.

Other published materials support Bishop Vargas's view that a search for a reconciliation vocabulary was in the air. In a short summary, the Sodalitium Vitae journal *FE* (1986, vi) reported: "The goal of the meeting was to study the Pope's thoughts on reconciliation and to deepen in modern man [*sic*], made in the image and likeness of God—and separated from their Creator by sin—the aspiration for a sincere and lasting reconciliation." Thus, by the mid-1980s, the stage was set for presenting the Latin American Church with a theological vocabulary alternative to that of liberation theology. And when Bishop Vargas Ruíz de Somocurcio presented the pope with the first working document on reconciliation, the gesture symbolized the Catholic right's major offensive against liberation theology in Peru. Following the already imposed censure of liberation theology by the Vatican, reconciliation provided a model of theology that Latin American conservative bishops were prepared to embrace.

Bishop Vargas emphasized that what he and others wanted most for the Peruvian Church was unity:

> Not that we all think alike or have the same ideas or follow similar theological currents, but we shouldn't take away one fundamental idea, and that is unity of faith, charity, or the love which should bring us together. . . . Undoubtedly today in the Church and in Peru, as you must already know, there are different theological currents—new movements that have emerged. . . . I wish these could come together. The Church is one. . . . I feel we've been missing this. (1988a)

Clearly, for the bishop as well as for others, the theology of reconciliation filled a void. That is why the issue here is not whether the concept of reconciliation was good or bad; for some, the theology of reconciliation did fill a void in a country where liberation had come to mean revolution, violence, and death. But one cannot ignore the fact that the idea for a theology of reconciliation came at a very critical moment for the Latin American Catholic right.

Mobilizing for Success

At the 1979 CELAM conference in Puebla, Mexico, the Catholic right was suspect, primarily because its representatives did all they could to marginalize Father Gustavo Gutiérrez and the other liberation theologians. Those efforts did not fully succeed, because even John Paul II, who had cautioned those present against some aspects of liberation theology, concluded that the Catholic Church did have a moral obligation to side with the poor. The pope's tepid attitude toward liberation theology from 1979 onward, however, provided an opportunity for broadened opposition to liberationists, and conservative groups took advantage of that opportunity. The 1985 Sodalitium Vitae conference on reconciliation, for example, came on the heels of the Vatican's publication of Ratzinger's (1984)

"Instruction on Certain Aspects of the Theology of Liberation," which the Catholic right took as its seal of approval to go after the liberationists, both internationally and nationally. The conference was also timely for the simple fact that it gave legitimacy to an already energized conservative constituency's attacks on advocates of liberation theology.

Those on the right argued that Sodalitium Vitae offered an ideal program for Peru: the political crises in the region had created an air of urgency, and what Sodalitium Vitae was providing after years of political chaos was a message of peace. Many who were equating liberation theology with Marxism and even with leftist armed revolutions saw in the message of reconciliation an alternative to violence. For those genuinely tired of conditions in Peru, the message seemed to promise peace and an end to violence. But right-wing politicians, the upper classes, and conservative bishops opposed to liberation saw in the theology of reconciliation a way to turn popular sentiment away from the theology of liberation. The theology of reconciliation, as the pope had written it and as Figari was interpreting it, retained one important element of liberationism: a social justice theme—but in a form that could be popular among the poor without the political implications inherent in liberation theology. Yet clearly, to achieve the transformation from liberation to reconciliation theology, proponents had to reach the masses. And to do that, they had to bring one particular segment of the Catholic Church on board—the pastoral agents.

Pastoral agents, though often neglected in discussions of Church history and often marginalized within the Church itself, are probably among the most important figures in Catholic proselytizing because, as noted earlier, they are the laypeople assigned to teach Church doctrine wherever there are shortages of priests. Their power lies in the fact that in Peru, for example, they are sent out to work in the *pueblos jovenes,* base Christian communities, and other Church programs beyond the reach of an ever diminishing Catholic priesthood. Thus, in times of ideological crisis or debate, the hierarchy must turn to them to reaffirm, realign, or change theological messages.

Bishop Vargas of Arequipa (1988a) has described their importance:

> I believe the pastoral agents should first of all shape the church, that is, shape community. Sometimes shaping community is understood as forming an elite of chosen ones. Forming community, however, encompasses everything: all social levels, all cultural spheres, and those things that pull us together—through unity in God and faith. It should be a unity that is translated into a concern for man [sic]. John Paul II frequently talked about concerns for mankind, the meaning of Christ, and the Church, which were the three points covered in his discourse at Puebla. This is what we should bring into our practice, a concern for forming community. We should center ourselves in the person of Christ, the source of life. . . . We should focus not only on spirituality but on all aspects of it, especially in areas where there is deep poverty—where many of our pastoral agents work. . . . They feel that everyone has an obligation, an obligation to shape their communities and to do something for their communities, whether making bricks to build a children's food kitchen or [establishing] a shelter for the aged. They are members of small communities who understand that if they seed these deep feelings, then the projects and work will take off on their own.

Clearly, the bishop felt that poor communities were entitled to address their needs through community projects, but he was also firmly against confusing community activism with political activism. The Catholic right at the time had to find a way to get that message out. And tackling liberationists from the top down was simply not going to be as effective as working directly with local parishes and base Christian communities.

The concept of the pastoral agent had emerged in the heyday of Vatican II as a way to make the laity a more integral part of the Church. More important, the role of pastoral agents in parishes and in base Christian communities was expanded primarily in response to the declining numbers of men entering the Catholic priesthood. Thus, the Bishop of Arequipa was quite correct in his assessment that he and groups such as Sodalitium Vitae ought to be involved in their training, for influencing pastoral agents meant influencing the organization and the activities of base Christian communities—which had often modeled themselves after liberation theology ideals.

Clearly, then, for the Church hierarchy to be successful in turning the tide on a mass scale, it needed to convert the pastoral agents from a theology of liberation to a theology of reconciliation. This is why the first strategy of the reconciliationists involved conferences on reconciliation.

At the 1985 conference, according to the Bishop of Arequipa, who hosted it, the largest number of participants were pastoral agents. At issue was the need to provide a theological model that both addressed poverty and offered an alternative to armed dissent. Reconciliationists clearly understood that quieting the masses required them to recognize the economic needs of the masses. No message of reconciliation would be successful if it did not make poor people's concerns central to its theology.

Bishop Vargas (1988a) provided insight into how the "ethic of charity" was shaping community projects in his diocese.

> We sometimes need to do for them [the poor] what they cannot do for themselves. Sometimes the government does not have the capacity to do it either, and we should be prepared to provide people with help either from foreign Catholic institutions or other groups, not necessarily Catholic, that can help us with ma-

terials to build a life with dignity: water, drainage, walkways, roads—the fundamentals. We could create centers for artisans. There is a large weaving center here in Arequipa. These things help to provide skills for people of these communities. In small parishes, with the help of the "Club de Madres" [mother's group], women work from their homes and help themselves. They are making a contribution, and at the same time they help themselves without having to wait for handouts. . . . For these reasons we need everyone's participation in supporting these efforts.

The Clubs de Madres, as one type of self-help organization, financially support themselves for the most part but receive funding at the local bishop's discretion. They and similar organizations have been important in the popular sectors' mobilization of Church resources. Nationally, these locally based organizations have been considered integral to the empowerment of the popular sector. They form part of a larger network of community organizations that support food kitchens (*comedores*) in both marginalized urban and depressed rural areas of Peru (Cordova 1989, 65). Their projects have generated jobs in child care, education, health, and food programs in the *pueblos jovenes*. Members of the Clubs de Madres, for example, elect *socias* (associates), who, after training with El Programa de Asistencia Directa (PAD, or Direct Assistance Program, and showing proficiency as *animadoras* (mobilizers), are hired as teachers by the Ministry of Education (Cordova 1989, 70).

Food kitchens too have been integral to the survival strategies of many poor communities throughout Peru. These *comedores* grew out of school and health programs in the 1950s, which were funded primarily with U.S. aid (Villón 1989, 49). But in the 1960s they became more autonomous and were run primarily by such groups as the Clubs de Madres. The Church's role has been to support these programs through its Catholic relief organization, Cáritas (Villón 1989, 49). Bishop Durand estimated that between the months of August and December in 1988, Cáritas donations reached approximately three million people, about 50,000 in Callao, Lima, alone.

Reconciliationists and Cáritas Peru

After Vatican II, many parishes reformed their catechetical programs to include an emphasis on charity (Klaiber 1988, 45). Parochial schools worldwide collected money for Catholic missions, which included Catholic schools in Peru, where donations were earmarked for social programs in the *pueblos jovenes*.

Cáritas Peru, established in 1954, described itself in a 1990 internal report (not published) as the social programs arm of the Catholic Church. It saw its mission in training pastoral agents and in providing infrastructural support for individuals and organizations that promoted social programs. Its members regarded their organization as a way of strengthening community projects in the popular sector. Their programs included funding food kitchens, operating the Vaso de Leche ("glass of milk") program and providing construction materials for victims of earthquakes, floods, mud slides, and other natural disasters.

According to the same 1990 internal report, Cáritas had by then contributed to forty-one dioceses throughout Peru, primarily through its food, health, and emergency programs. It also sponsors regional meetings, workshops, publications, national and international conferences, courses, and other events that help it maintain strong ties with other Cáritas organizations internationally. In Peru, 75 to 85 percent of the donated food distributed among the different social programs comes from international organizations (Lizarzaburu 1989, 24), and Cáritas has become a centerpiece of those social programs. It is considered a benign form of social activism, precisely because it fits in well with the Church's support of programs that tend to remain dissociated from political activism (at least the Catholic hierarchy tries to keep it that way).

The history of Cáritas in Peru reflects that tendency. Cáritas Peru emerged at the time when the mass migrations to urban areas were forming what many have referred to as the "belts of poverty" surrounding Lima and other cities along the coast. Those demographic changes forced the Catholic Church to take notice of the structural crises that the massive migrations from the sierras were causing (Klaiber 1988, 347). And as the changing social fabric of Peru forced upper-class Peruvians and elite institutions to reckon with the changes, liberals and progressives in the Catholic Church began to respond by becoming more actively involved in the day-to-day life of the growing *pueblos jovenes*. "The source of material support for missionary work in the *barriadas* was Cáritas International, which had in 1954 established an office in Peru. Cáritas channeled many of the contributions that were coming from organizations like Catholic Relief Service of the United States to the Church's centers in the poor barrios" (Klaiber 1988, 348).

For some, Cáritas Peru was limiting because it espoused a message of charity without offering any real critique of Peruvian society and the causes of poverty. But Bishop Durand, who has served as its president, and others working in the reconciliationist vein saw its mission as consistent with the goals of the theology of reconciliation. According to Bishop Durand (1991):

> There are two sides to the struggle under way here that are giving us catastrophic results—the first is Sendero, and the second is MRTA [Movimiento Revolucionario Túpac Amaru]—because they destroy more where there is the most misery. Either we help people to keep hope and avoid the type of conflict that worsens

the situation, or we go the route of reconciliation with a hope to go on. That is why we have the food kitchens. We are serving more than 190,000 people, at really low fees, and our serving capacity can reach 250,000. . . . Other educational and vocational centers now reach 10,000 to 11,000 people. Our hope is to give them skills so that their labor will provide more for them. . . . It is a practical way of giving to the hungry, providing health needs, in order to help them—as Pope Paul VI said in "Populorum Progressio"—to be agents of their own progress.

But critics have argued that one limitation of programs such as the *comedores* is that most of them rely on donations and thus perpetuate poor people's economic dependency on international organizations. Many of the bishops who control the community projects that are chiefly funded by Cáritas donations feel threatened by local grassroots leadership, particularly in the base communities, and tend to crack down on any sign of autonomy in these community-based programs. A representative of Cáritas Peru who did not want to be identified agreed that this was a problem and said that Cáritas, acknowledging those criticisms, is trying to make the programs more empowering to the communities. But for reconciliationists and the Catholic right in general, these charitable operations remain the programs of choice, because they can meet the needs of the poor without promoting political activism.

It should be noted that Cáritas does not represent the voice of either reconciliationists or liberationists per se; instead, it maintains a neutral position in matters of theology. But it is clear that as a Catholic organization subject to the whims of the Church hierarchy, Cáritas and its programs often become tools of the bishops who control diocesan activities. Several former workers in Cáritas programs who were interviewed for this book said they were pushed out by bishops who labeled them Marxists or political activists.

The Catholic right has often expressed publicly its fear of Marxist influences reaching the *pueblos jovenes* projects. Bishop Vargas, for example, in the speech quoted previously (1988b) spoke of "authors characterized by their conflictual orientation, predominantly political, who are the principal exponents of said Marxist analysis" and labeled Gustavo Gutiérrez "a leader in that orientation, which the Vatican . . . called erroneous and bad for the faith." Critics of Sodalitium Vitae say that Vargas's statement represents what is truly at the heart of the movement's mission—to go after Father Gutiérrez, liberation theology, and anything deemed leftist. They hold that the Sodalitium Vitae movement has been nothing more than a well-orchestrated attempt to undermine the revolutionary processes that have shaped and continue to shape Latin America today. One article charged that the leaders of this attempt "have only recycled old ideas and that their ideological offensives are clear. Their positions can be clearly seen in the reappearance of reactionary publications, which are circulating throughout Peru [and have] . . . brought a type of nostalgia to the high Limeñan bourgeoisie" (*Marka* 1975).

Opus Dei versus Liberationist Reform

One can argue that the Catholic right is determined to return once again to a Church entrenched in tradition, official and orthodox in its theological formulas, and fixated on juridical-canonical aspects of the liturgy (Boff 1985, 2–3). A document circulated in 1987 by Opus Dei Archbishop Orbegozzo typifies the kinds of measures the Catholic right is willing to take in establishing its control. Orbegozzo decreed a major restructuring of parish activities in the diocese of Chiclayo, which he justified by appealing to Church law. Among his instructions as to the manner in which parish business would be conducted, the archbishop ordered

- that the parish priest study and evaluate pastoral activities and . . . approve [or disapprove] any decisions concerning them;
- that the parish priest consider with knowledge and prudence any ideas presented to him, to the end that this will help him effect a better-governed parish;
- that the parish priest oversee the number of members elected to the parish council and that, before he allows individuals to take office, their names be presented to the diocesan bishop for confirmation;
- that in the event the parish priest is replaced, the parish council present their resignations to the new parish priest, who may or may not confirm their reappointment;
- that the parish council retain no responsibilities regarding these decisions; it does have a moral responsibility to advise with good conscience, but ultimately, final decisions remain in the hands of the parish priest, the one responsible, as pastor, for the saving of souls;
- and, finally, that all pastoral groups look to the parish council for guidance. (Orbegozzo 1987b)

The archbishop was clear in his objectives. Each item in the document underscored the central role of the priest and emphasized the secondary role of the parish council. And to assure his own control over the parishes under his jurisdiction, he ordered that each parish priest seek diocesan approval for projected parish activities.

The archbishop's intentions had been in the making years before these orders were made public. Several congregations (branches of religious orders) had resigned their posts in his diocese because their projects were being radically altered. A number of the Church personnel working in the area revealed in interviews that they had quit or had been forced out of the diocese by Archbishop Orbegozzo. Just as in other instances already mentioned, priests and other Church personnel who were not willing to adhere to his instructions were subject to censure or relocation. Bishops were authorized to carry out such actions, and they often did so without allowing debate.

The consequences have had political ramifications, even though Opus Dei members have stated repeatedly that politics and religion should not mix. Whatever their response to crisis situations, community projects, and demands for participatory democracy in parish affairs, it has become clear that whether Church officials in Peru admit it or not, they often align their theological positions with their political ones. For example, the first volume of *Antología de Textos,* a publication overseen by Father Ramon Rocca Salles (1985) with the official support of Archbishop Orbegozzo, was dedicated to pointing out the errors of what Opus Dei saw as a Marxist-based theology. Similarly, incidents such as the expulsion of striking teachers from the cathedral in Chiclayo clearly revealed Opus Dei as a conservative organization and occasionally exposed its members' political bias against popular protests. An article in *Marka* (1975) titled "La Derecha en la Iglesia" (The right in the Church) concluded:

> There are some institutions or groups of the "right" who work actively in the Church. Until now the activities they support in Peru have had a nonpublic, not to mention clandestine, character. For the most part, their members publicly deny membership in these organized groups. The few who do show their faces reiterate the nonpolitical character of said institutions, and they cling to explanations of their activities in strictly religious or pastoral terms. But their actions display the opposite.

At least one difference between Opus Dei and the liberationists is their view of the Church's relationship to the different classes of people. One Church activist commented:

You can see their [Opus Dei members'] closeness to the middle and upper classes. Just look at where they focus their resources. Look at where they build their cultural houses [in the richest sectors of cities and towns], how they build them [with significantly more extravagance than the average Peruvian home], and who goes to their meetings [well-connected, professional, and upper-class persons]. You see how the Opus Dei priest is turned into the administrator of the sacrament; they don't look for ways to get close to the people. They are the ones who run the parish rather than enabling people and working with them to be leaders of their own community.

Other activists argued that the leaders of Opus Dei lean toward vertical paternalistic relations, often citing their founder's ideas as fundamental truths, with little or no debate. Their approach to poverty is based on traditional understandings of "good works," particularly in the *pueblos jovenes* and rural peasant communities.

Interviews with Church activists illustrated the frustration that they had others experienced in the Opus Dei–controlled diocese of Chiclayo, partly because of their disagreement with the way Opus Dei channels diocesan resources. The expenditure most commented on was the construction of a monastic sanctuary to honor the Virgin Mary. According to a pamphlet circulated at the Chiclayo Cathedral in the Plaza de Armas, the idea for the sanctuary began in February 1985 when Pope John Paul II blessed the Virgin's statue before 25,000 Chiclayans, and a local Opus Dei priest said the effort was meant to "promote a public veneration of Our Lady of Peace." The care and maintenance of the sanctuary would be assigned to a group of contemplative women religious of the Spanish Carmelite Order. But for Church workers in the popular sector, the sanctuary project exemplified the rift between Opus Dei interests and their own, and it sharpened the differences between the diocesan hierarchy and proponents of liberation theology. According to one informant, Opus Dei's basic inter-action with the *pueblos jovenes* was simply at the level of pro-viding traditional Church services—the mass, baptism, and so on: "Opus Dei priests administer the sacraments and provide religious services to the poor in some of their *pueblos jovenes,* while they also take up collections to house and honor a statue of the Virgin Mary of Peace, leaving the poor without adequate housing or homeless."

Professor Luz Gonzalez (1988) vice-rector of the Univer-sity of Piura and a leader of the women's sector of Opus Dei, challenged that assessment, saying that students at the uni-versity engineer projects for local poor communities: she cited housing construction and ways of using cheap, efficient fuels. Other students were assigned to teach health care, nutrition, and farming techniques. But, community activists argued, the issue was not so much what they did but rather how they as-sessed and decided on community needs: the activists felt that Opus Dei leaders set up projects according to what *they* con-sidered to be in the best interest of the communities. These top-down decisions made clear to Church community activists the Catholic right's lack of concern for the input of the popu-lar sector.

This attitude toward the poor is consistent with Opus Dei beliefs, because theirs is a traditionalism reminiscent of the years before the restructuring of the Church that came with the changes of Vatican II. Despite those changes, Opus Dei has been given new life because there "is a sense that Pope John Paul II has put a stop to interpreting liberally the documents of the Second Vatican Council and that a new era of conserva-tism has begun" (Kamm 1984, 84). Thus, Opus Dei, Sodali-tium Vitae, and other right-wing Catholic groups have become powerful forces in the Latin American Catholic Church be-cause the Church hierarchy as it stands today supports their right to determine activities in their parishes. This model of the Church has restricted the activity of popular groups; the pope, the bishops, and the general hierarchical structure have come to constitute the organizational axis for defining the Church as "essentially clerical," for "without the clergy nothing decisive can happen within the community"; Church teachings are interpreted rigidly, and "the Church's vision becomes legalistic, confined to those in positions of power within the Church" (Boff 1985, 3–4). Archbishop Orbegozzo's actions against the SUTEP strikers in 1979 and his published policies in 1987, Bishop Durand's open attack against leftist and progressive religious personnel in Callao, Lima, and a whole series of actions by the right were evidence that the Catholic right was effectively reasserting itself in Peru.

The themes exploited in the theology of reconciliation came at a time when conservatives needed to fulfill an ideological need for the Church to voice concern for the poor while continuing to assert its hold on tradition and authority. At a 1988 bishops' conference in Venezuela, Bishop Vargas's paper "Liberación y Reconciliación en America Latina" (Liberation and reconciliation in Latin America) provided insight into the Catholic right's view of the issues: "Latin Americans are part of the Third World, but [there are] many who cannot advance their own efficient means for solutions; others have greater influence . . . but are little interested in cooperating with the improvement of the circumstances which oppress the men and women of our countries" (1988b, 1). Vargas rejected the liberationist model as a solution, however, and called on his colleagues for alternative solutions.

Figari, representing the reconciliationist view, made one position clear when he described "the character of spirituality for our time" at a conference on spirituality held at his pastoral center in Monterrico, Lima, in February 1988: "First, everyone must direct his or her life to the Father [*sic*] in Christ: aspiring to organic unity with God, a loving obedience to God's plan, a mystic life in God, all of which leads to the resolution of conflict through reconciliation." Although his ideas fell short of a specific plan for resolving social problems, they had particular appeal among traditionalists and conservatives, who clearly rejected mass-based political actions.

Factions within Factions

The ecclesial directory of Peru (*Directorio* 1987, 584) reported twenty priests to be members of Opus Dei. Of the three bishops earlier identified as Opus Dei members (*Directorio* 1984), none had posts in Lima, where the power base of the Peruvian hierarchy was centered. On the other hand, the Sodalitium Vitae was almost exclusively based in Lima.

At the same time, by contrast, open supporters of liberation theology among bishops and priests were more numerous and geographically widespread. Membership in ONIS, for example, was a good indication of priests' sympathy to liberation theology; an article attacking ONIS for its proximity to Marxism documented approximately 102 priests as supporters (*Realidad* 1979). Members of ONIS also represented almost every province in Peru; some held university positions or directed institutes or both, but most worked in popular sectors.

Further, the number of participants at the annual summer theology course sponsored by the Theology Department of the Catholic University reached a high of 2,502 in 1986, but even that figure did not reflect the total number of pastoral agents in Peru who were using liberation theology in their basic teaching. The fact that approximately 102 priests were available resources to these constituencies and were active in almost every province suggests that the support for liberation theology was even higher than conference participation indicated and broader than the support reported by the ecclesial directory for Sodalitium Vitae or Opus Dei.

In 1986 a list of possible candidates for the post of Archbishop of Lima, published by the news magazine *Visión Peruana,* revealed that the competition between supporters of Sodalitium Vitae and Opus Dei and proponents of liberation theology is not only over theology but over high levels of Church influence and resources:

> Liberationists and conciliators have initiated a conclave to define the future of the ecclesial character of the next Archbishopric of Lima. Some 60 bishops of the Peruvian Episcopate will have to decide sooner or later which among them will replace [soon to retire] Cardinal Juan Landázuri—a central figure of influence in the nation's life since 1954. . . . Among the potential successors there are five bishops who have worked closely with Landázuri to understand the problems of Lima. . . . Three of them openly subscribe to liberation theology, and the other two do not oppose it.

On the opposite side were listed three important figures who make up the greatest threat to liberation theology and each of whom publicly supports the theology of reconciliation: Bishops Durand, Vargas Alzamora, and Vargas of Arequipa.

> Bishop Durand Flores is widely known in Lima. He is perhaps one of the bishops who can forcefully defend his point of view. . . . He is one of the promoters of the theology of reconciliation and totally rejects the one on liberation. . . . Vargas Alzamora [already second in command to Landázuri] may possibly have the capacity to be the ecclesial converging point [and] . . . be elected to the presidency [of the Peruvian Episcopate]. . . . Bishop Fernando Vargas of Arequipa, a friend of Landázuri, is the candidate of the reconciliation proponents. . . . His supporters, in citing Church tradition dating to the *virreinato* [colonial period], consider that as Archbishop of Arequipa, he should have the Archbishopric of Lima. (*Visión Peruana* 1986)

In the end, Augusto Vargas Alzamora replaced Juan Landazuri Ricketts as Archbishop of Lima.

One should not assume, however, that the only division in Church affairs was between a unified liberation theology and a monolithic conservative movement. For example, the theme of reconciliation made some inroads into liberationism's support base. Bishop Bambaren of Chimbote, once an advocate of liberation theology, is among those who have modified their stance:

> I think there is an important role the Church can play . . . as mediator. When the Church mediates, groups in conflict normally respond, which doesn't happen when other authorities mediate. For example, in the case of the fishermen's strike here . . . I said to both sides that the riches of the sea are for everyone. It is clear that no one here planted or cultivated anything, so, I proposed a question for discussion. I asked them if they agreed that the catches should benefit all the groups. They agreed. Using that question-and-answer strategy, I was able to help them see that no one should benefit at the expense of the other. . . . And on the basis of such exchanges, many problems have been resolved. . . . In the resolution of the strike there were two agreements reached: that the riches of the sea shouldn't benefit only the groups involved in its commerce; rather they should help the poor sectors of the community too. Consequently, the St. Peter's Social Fund was formed, which . . . doesn't benefit any interest group more than another, but more the poor who work at the ports. Also, an Honor Tribunal was formed, organized by officials of the fishing industries, unions, and other vested parties. All these groups asked that the tribunal be put under the direction of the Church. It meets once a month and has become a point of convergence and dialogue for the parties involved. (1988)

Echoing Bishop Bambaren's view, Bishop Dammert Bellido (1988) commented: "The Church has to collaborate in solving some of Peru's problems, because it is intimately tied to justice, charity, and the defense of human rights; therefore, the

Church must make itself present. In many instances it is the only institution that has credibility among the people, because of disappointments people have had to endure from politics and politicians."

Although Bishop Bambaren's actions in 1971 symbolized a Church willing to legitimate the issues of the popular sector, he now cautions against the divisive debates over liberation theology: "We must be careful not to fall into the trap of being polarized by being for or against liberation theology. . . . You can lose perspective and get lost in the debate. . . . There is an important task that must take place that is the process of clarification, . . . of making the language explicit, that has been done. Gustavo [Father Gustavo Gutiérrez] himself has done this too" (1988).

Similarly, though Opus Dei and Sodalitium Vitae are often in agreement, it is important to note their differences. Sodalitium Vitae was better positioned to create an effective movement toward conservatism because unlike Opus Dei, its leadership emerged from a Latin American cultural base, not a European one: its founder was Peruvian, and the members of the Church hierarchy who supported it came from either Peru or neighboring countries.

This cultural base reflects what mobilization theorists have observed as the basis of successful resource mobilization. "The broad factors within a population affecting its degree of mobilization [include] the extent of its shared interest in interactions with other populations" (Tilly 1978, 81). The result of successful mobilization by the Catholic right in the mid-1980s was documented by newspaper reports that when more than three hundred bishops participated in a theological congress in Caracas, Venezuela, in February 1988, they examined "themes linked to liberation theology, a perspective based on Marxist ideas, which, . . . despite a world full of faults, was an unacceptable theory" (*El Comercio* 1988).

For theological ideas to succeed in mobilizing large groups of people around this sort of sentiment, they must resonate with a cultural base where the theology can thrive. Whereas Opus Dei theology has represented colonial traditionalism, Sodalitium Vitae represents the emergence of an indigenous-based Catholic conservatism. It came to have broader appeal in Peru because it took into account the political character of Peruvian society. In short, it provides an alternative not only to liberation theology but also to Opus Dei ideology. Sodalitium Vitae evolved in such a way that it built a distinctly Latin American, conservative power base. It gave a whole new focus to Catholic conservatism in Peru, without the pre–Vatican II provincialism that was embedded in the heart and soul of Opus Dei.

As a former member recalled, apparently Opus Dei "wanted to preserve everything the colonial church had imposed in Peru. When they [Opus Dei priests] serve communion, they don't give it to you in the hand [as post–Vatican II rituals encourage]. They focus on tradition, wear the more traditional priests' vestments, and they still use Latin during mass." Not serving communion in the hand was seen by opponents of Opus Dei as symbolic of the hierarchical relationship remaining between the priest and the lay community. As the informant suggested, the laity were seen by Opus Dei as unworthy of touching "holy" symbols and unauthorized to share in priestly functions. Members of Opus Dei often charged that the changes begun by Vatican II had sparked an undermining of priests' authority; opponents responded that Opus Dei priests rejected the changes brought on by Vatican II because they wanted to maintain a hierarchical system that distanced itself from the masses and their socio-economic problems.

Sodalitium Vitae, on the other hand, became attractive to a Latin American Catholic right that had not only adopted basic Church reform but recognized the extent to which liberation theology had influenced the Church. In Figari's words:

> From the start, we were deeply marked by the Second Vatican Council. Medellín, with its ideal of liberation as a deeply felt aspiration, influenced and expressed our style, our lives, and our actions—liberation in keeping with a Christian and ecclesial perspective. . . . We are convinced, however, that a liberation proposed and situated outside the teachings of the Church can only convert itself in new oppression. (1985, 22)

Thus, unlike Opus Dei, Sodalitium Vitae presents itself as sensitized to the Peruvian people and to Latin American social concerns in general. It also provides a sympathetic ear to issues of national concern, while at the same time rejecting liberation theology on the grounds that it crosses religious-political boundaries. This difference provides the Sodalitium Vitae movement with an advantage in Peru. Despite their differences, however, the two groups share two goals: to rid the Church of the liberationists, and to maintain a rigid hierarchical Catholic traditionalism.

Summary

The theology of reconciliation emerged as the discourse of the alternative ideology that fueled a countermovement to liberation theology: namely, the Sodalitium Vitae movement. This countermovement was an indirect effort to quiet the political upheaval that came to characterize Peru from the 1960s to the 1980s. Following the Vatican's censure of liberation theology in the mid-1980s, the theme of reconciliation—supported by conservative bishops and such existing groups as Opus Dei—became the impetus for an ideological revision of the liberation theme and the ethical rationale for the activism associated with that revision.

The theology of reconciliation proposed an alternative set of beliefs to liberation theology and the liberationist programs it had inspired within the Church. The conflicting perspectives underlying the two ideologies were grounded in a general ideological confrontation between supporters of the popular sector and a Catholic right that opposed their political agenda. The ability of the Catholic right to redirect the protest energy of the 1960s and 1970s into a quieting reformulation of liberation theology—in some instances by rhetorical persuasion and in other instances by force—suggests the limitations on the efforts of liberationists, tied to the same Church resources, to transform that Church. In other words, the censure, relocation, or expulsion of liberationists and the co-optation of liberation theology by other groups with comparable institutional power suggests the vulnerability of social movements with ties to the same organizational resources as their opponents. Countermovements too can use ideas and organizational resources to mobilize formidable attacks on their opposition. Here, not only was the concept of reconciliation important in mobilizing the Catholic right, but the Church hierarchy with its vast institutional power helped advance the Sodalitium Vitae cause.

Epilogue

F ew in Peru would argue that the Catholic Church is less than complex, and most would agree that it is certainly divided when it comes to politics. This book's examination of these conflicting positions provides a context in which to analyze the debate over liberation theology in Peru and, more generally, in Latin America as a whole.

A key part of the relationship between the popular sectors of Peru and proponents of liberation theology was the ability of liberation theology's proponents to espouse an ideological position compatible with that of other like-minded groups. How they did so is crucial to an understanding of the processes by which intellectuals become useful to social movements. In this case, those who became liberation theologians were transformed by the set of historical circumstances that characterized the political life of Peru from the late 1950s to the 1970s and by the fact that the Catholic Church was not responding effectively to the growing mass of popular discontent. Consequently, many liberation theologians opted for different types of action. Father Camilo Torres of Colombia chose revolution;

Father Gustavo Gutiérrez worked toward reform of the Church and society.

It is important to note that the liberation theologians filled a void in the Church because the protest language of liberation theology gave voice to an already mobilized popular sector that was attracting Christian social activists. The liberation theologians were successful in their role as intellectuals mainly because they provided "the kind of ideological package that successfully resonated with larger cultural themes" (Gamson 1988, 227). This ability to resonate with poor people's movements gave these liberationist intellectuals an important role in mobilizing support for the popular sector in Peru, primarily because they were able to galvanize and focus sentiment on the status and living conditions of poor people. By working in the *pueblos jovenes* and creating institutional space for network organizing around this sentiment, they legitimized the Christian activists' place within the protest movements of the popular sector. And more important, the theological call for solidarity with the poor provided new mobilizing possibilities for the popular sectors as they turned to the Church for support. Even when popular protest strategies began to include church takeovers and land squatting on Church property, the protesters found support among liberal-to-leftist Catholic priests, sisters, and laypeople.

The institutional support that poor people's movements received from advocates of liberation theology was based on a common belief that the status of poor people in Peru and elsewhere in Latin America was both unjust and antithetical to biblical teachings. Thus, the mind-set that came to characterize liberation theology produced not only verbal solidarity with poor people's struggles but also organizational network support for popular causes.

In Peru, the inspiration for the kind of Christian social

activism that came to flower because of liberation theology depended on the priest-theologian Gustavo Gutiérrez. Father Gutiérrez provided not only a set of guiding principles that called for solidarity with the poor but also a number of organizational outlets that encouraged network activity and helped to bring the plight of poor people to national and international attention. The institutes that he co-founded in Lima, the Bartolomé de Las Casas Institute and the Center for Research and Publication, disseminated information about liberation theology through their publications and also provided organizational space for a number of groups and scholars to come together. Professors from various universities were encouraged to collaborate there in research that touched on issues concerning the poor. The Catholic University's annual theology workshops permitted an even broader audience—comprising both national and international supporters of liberation theology—to exchange ideas and to influence Gutiérrez's writings. While he was actually building the liberation theology movement, the fact that he was an internationally respected scholar, a priest who worked in the *pueblos jovenes,* and the national director of the Catholic Action student organization UNEC allowed him to exploit the kind of social location within a social movement community that is essential to recruitment, dissemination of information, and expansion of movement opportunities.

Gutiérrez's former ties to Catholic Action organizations gave him instant access to a population of liberal-to-radical Catholics open to expanding theological ideas beyond the political scope of Catholic Action. Catholic Action had become limited in scope primarily because it came out of a tradition that tended to reject socialist influences. Vatican II changed that attitude by taking the position that there was nothing to be feared from Marxist-Christian dialogues. Consequently, groups of priests who were already involved in such dialogues could openly discuss their views, and many of them adopted versions of liberation theology in line with the idea that there was much to be gained in using Marxist analysis when talking about the status of poor people in Latin America. The priest division of ONIS evolved out of that theological perspective. As Vidales (1993) noted, ONIS was important because its member priests not only organized people in Peru but were often called upon to advise groups outside Peru.

As Gutiérrez worked to develop his brand of liberation theology, he was helped by the network environment that evolved around him, the poor parish where he worked, the institutes he cofounded, his encounters with Christian activists and pastoral agents from the *pueblos jovenes,* and the university settings he frequented; all these played a part in shaping what today is known as the theology of liberation. Yet despite the appeal of liberation theology, its rejection by the Catholic right eventually imposed severe limitations on its activities. This turn of events suggests the vulnerability of reformist movements in instances where countermovements are in a position to compete for the same organizational resources and the same audiences.

Catholic conservatives saw popular protest and the kind of participatory democracy that came to characterize base Christian communities as threats to the authority of the Church hierarchy. Consequently, the Catholic right mobilized against those groups, arguing against any social activism that involved church takeovers, land squatting, or a protest strategy that had the potential to escalate into the violence that was contrary to official Catholic teachings. The Catholic right used its power within the Church to reorganize base Christian communities by mobilizing conservative bishops who saw such organizational structures as an affront to their authority; many bishops in Central and South America came out against liberation theology.

The most visible member of the Latin American Church hierarchy to launch an open attack on the liberation theologians, their adherents, and the programs they inspired was Cardinal Alfonso López Trujillo of Colombia. He and his recruits reorganized parishes and expelled noncomplying clergy and laypeople from Church dioceses. More important, they brought their issues before the 1979 CELAM conference and won over a number of influential bishops. Crowning the cardinal's efforts a few years later was support from the Vatican, which gave the Catholic right in Latin America the institutional support it needed to make its countermovement even more effective. As retrenchment policies began to take hold, they forced a number of liberationist priests and sisters to leave the Church because they found themselves censured, reassigned, or pushed out of parish decision-making. Two of the more noted figures who left the Church because of the unrelenting attack by the Catholic right were Ernesto Cardenal of Nicaragua and Leonardo Boff of Brazil.

It was in that political environment that the Sodalitium Vitae movement emerged and found support—though small at first—both inside and outside Peru. Like the liberationists, its adherents created an organizational base from which to exercise their opposition to poor people's movements. With the support of Bishops Durand, Vargas of Arequipa, Vargas Alzamora, and others, Sodalitium Vitae flourished and grew into a movement able to sponsor international conferences on reconciliation. The significance of these events lies in the fact that the panelists at the conferences represent ties to a national and international constituency which, though small, has been influential in attacking liberation theology; again, Cardinal López Trujillo of Colombia is the most notable example. These ties coupled with the organizational base that Sodalitium Vitae has been able to establish—by means of a pastoral center, publication facilities, connections with seminaries in Peru, Brazil, and El Salvador and with other conservative groups such as Opus Dei—suggest that Sodalitium Vitae will continue to exercise influence in Peru and beyond. And its attack on liberation theology will be successful so long as it can continue to tap institutional resources, retain mass appeal among adherents of the status quo, and use Latin America's continuing weariness with violence to the advantage of its emphasis on reconciliation.

Events in Peru and Latin America surrounding the debate over liberation theology suggest a dialectic that reflects the ability of one group to generate radical changes under one set of social circumstances and of another group, under new conditions, to challenge those changes. In Latin America opponents of liberation theology have been able to make the Marxist label stick and—by citing the civil wars in Nicaragua, Guatemala, Honduras, El Salvador, Colombia, and Peru—have been able to argue persuasively that revolutions upset poor people's lives rather than bringing solutions to their problems. Indications thus far suggest that people continue to want an end to violence. But their attraction to liberation theology has forced the Catholic right to recognize that any solution must take poor people's struggles into account.

What this book has not addressed is the status of liberation theology today as a result of the efforts of the Catholic right. Or, to put the question more accurately, has the status quo altered the course of liberation theology in Peru and Latin America? The outcome of the controversy will depend on the Latin American people themselves. The debate over liberation theology is not limited to the interests of a Catholic status quo. It involves a majority of people whose economic and political reality is not that of Latin America's elites. In other words, even though conservative bishops such as Durand, Vargas, and Orbegozzo all have powerful allies outside Peru and the support of the Vatican, the political power of the poor in history suggests that what happens to liberation theology will not depend simply on what the Catholic right wants for Latin America.

If anything, the history of popular movements in Peru and Latin America shows that when the right does successfully co-opt and harness protest movements, it can do so only for a time. During my fieldwork for this book, I noted that despite the Catholic right's effort to eradicate progressive-to-radical parish activities, the people were continuing with their projects wherever the resolve to continue seemed strong. That is to say, in a number of instances neither bishops nor priests were successful in stopping such activities: the people continued doing their work, clandestinely if necessary. The existence of that phenomenon suggests that future study in this area may need new ways of measuring the success of the countermovement against liberation theology at the grassroots level. Perhaps books written ten, twenty, or more years from now will be telling of the continuing success or the resurgence of liberation theology in Latin America, despite the retrenchment policies that at present have put it under attack. For now, it seems that a severe blow has been dealt—but the extent of its impact is yet to be fully assessed, and certainly the extent of liberation theology's staying power is yet to be discovered.

The significance of this discussion lies in highlighting the important role that intellectuals and ideologies can play in mobilizing sentiment and social movement resources within the changing tides of political climates. The story of the theology of liberation, though unfinished, demonstrates that intellectuals can become dynamic forces of social change, particularly when they use their skills to help foster the kind of sentiment that can lead to mobilizing organizational resources for any given social movement. Father Gutiérrez and others were successful at exercising extensive influence over members of the Church hierarchy, universities, local parishes, and a network of international supporters. The liberationist influence sometimes led to unexpected support for the popular sector in labor and land disputes. Gutiérrez's brand of liberation theology mobilized the kind of sentiment necessary for bringing together otherwise seemingly dissimilar groups of protesters.

Thus, it is important to note that although ideas and intellectuals do not necessarily create social movements, they do play an integral role in social movements by articulating and elaborating broader movement sentiments that others may find appealing—whether for a progressive or conservative cause. The success of both the liberation and reconciliation theologians' abilities to bridge, at times, seemingly distinct groups depended upon their ability to frame a compelling theological model. Liberationists brought together social activists motivated by religious moral outrage and others who defined themselves strictly in political terms but welcomed the support of any who shared their political views. Reconciliationists were able to mobilize support from both moderate conservative groups and traditionalists as extreme as Opus Dei.

The purpose of this book is not to illustrate the validity of specific religion-motivated actions but to focus on the role of intellectuals and their ideas as useful resources in the mobilization of social movements. Theologians, in their roles as intellectuals, produced an ideological bridge that served several protest populations. Some did so by providing Church activists with the rationale for supporting the activities of the popular sector; others, by providing traditionalists with the rationale to oppose them. Belief systems, such as those analyzed here as liberation theology and the theology of reconciliation, can shape the direction of people's movement choices. Belief systems also create potential for the formation of coalitions among distinct populations. Intellectuals can create the bridge between those varying populations by articulating ideological stances and interpretations that can bring such groups together. Intellectuals are most effective when they can use their social location within the larger society to their advantage. In doing so, they enhance their respective movements' mobilizing potential.

APPENDIX

Persons Interviewed

Alvarez Calderón, Jorge. Priest, leader in Catholic Worker movement in Peru.

Alyza, Adelaida. Professor of theology at the Catholic University of Lima and personal friend of Father Gustavo Gutiérrez.

Alzamora Revoredo, Oscar. Former Bishop of Tacna, who hosted one of the reconciliation conferences.

Ames, Rolando. Former senator of Peru, member of United Left Party, professor of political science at the Catholic University of Lima, and regular participant in discussion groups at the Bartolomé de Las Casas Institute.

Baertl Gomez, Jaime. Priest, member of Sodalitium Vitae, and organizer of conferences on reconciliation.

Bambaren Gastelumendi, Luis. Bishop of Chimbote and president of the Comisión Episcopal de Acción Social (CEAS).

Crespo Tarrero, Luis Fernando. Director of UNEC chapter and professor of theology at the Catholic University of Lima, personal friend of Father Gustavo Gutiérrez.

Dammert Bellido, José. Bishop of Cajamarca, vice-president of the Peruvian Episcopal Conference Directorate, supporter of liberation theology and noted for his work with the poor.

Durand Florez, Ricardo. Bishop of Callao, Lima.

Felipe Zegarra, Luis. Professor of theology and spiritual director at the Catholic University of Lima, parish priest in a *pueblo joven* in Callao, Lima.

Gonzalez Umeres, Luz. Vice-rector and professor of philosophy at the University of Piura, leader of the Opus Dei women's sector.

Gutiérrez Merino, Gustavo. Liberation theologian, cofounder of Bartolomé de Las Casas Institute, national director of UNEC.

Moliné, Jesus. Opus Dei priest and spiritual director at the University of Piura.

Navarra, José. Rector of the University of Piura.

Piqueiras, Manuel. Former member of Peru's House of Representatives, member of the United Left Party.

Purisaca, Fidel. Secretary to Archbishop Orbegozzo of Chiclayo.

Rocca Salles, Ramon. Opus Dei priest in Chiclayo, director of the Santo Toribio Seminary, Church overseer of the Opus Dei publication *Antología de Textos*.

Romero, Catalina. Director of the Bartolomé de Las Casas Institute, professor of sociology at the Catholic University of Lima.

Silva Santiesteban, Hernan. Professor of ethics at the Catholic University of Lima.

Trapasso, Rosa Dominga. Maryknoll sister, cofounder of Talitha Cumi, friend of Ivan Illich.

Vargas Ruíz de Somocurcio, Fernando. Archbishop of Arequipa, supporter of the Sodalitium Vitae movement.

Vidales, Rául. Sociologist and theologian, friend of Father Gustavo Gutiérrez, cofounder of the Bartolomé de Las Casas Institute.

Additional interviews were conducted with the following persons who requested that their identities not be revealed.

A former member of Opus Dei who served in the organization's women's section for eight years.

A former member of the women's section of Opus Dei.

A former Opus Dei member who served in the men's section when he was a college student.

A spokesperson for Opus Dei in the Women's Center at Chiclayo.

A member and organizer of SUTEP (the teachers' union) who participated in the strike of 1979.

A lay Church activist who works in one of Lima's *pueblos jovenes*.

A lay Church activist and organizer in one of Lima's *pueblos jovenes;* she served on the discussion committee for Gutiérrez's book *We Drink from Our Own Wells*.

A lay Church activist who works in a Chiclayo *pueblo joven*.

A Catholic sister who works in a Chiclayo *pueblo joven*.

A priest who works in a Lima *pueblo joven* and was a member of ONIS.

A priest who works in a *pueblo joven* outside of Lima.

A layperson who frequently attended talks at the Women's Center in Chiclayo.

A student at the Catholic University of Lima who is a member of Sodalitium Vitae.

A representative of Caritás Peru.

REFERENCES

Abell, Aaron I.
1963 *American Catholicism and Social Action.* Notre Dame: University of Notre Dame Press.

Alvarez Calderón, Jorge
1991 Interview with author, June 27.

Alyza, Adelaida
1988 Interview with author, January 14.

Alzamora Revoredo, Oscar
1991 Interview with author, July 18.

Ames, Rolando
1991 Interview with author, July 27.

Aptheker, Herbert
1970 *The Urgency of Marxist-Christian Dialogue.* New York: Harper & Row.

Astiz, Carlos
1969 *Pressure Groups and Power Elites in Peruvian Politics.* Ithaca: Cornell University Press.

Baertl, Father Jaime Gomez
1991 Interviews with author, July.

Bambaren Gastelumendi, Luis
1988 Interview with author, April 8.

Berryman, Phillip
1987 *Liberation Theology: Essential Facts about the Revolutionary Movement in Latin America and Beyond.* New York: Pantheon.

Boff, Leonardo
1985 *Church: Charism and Power.* New York: Crossroad.
1992 Communiqué to Associated Press, July 2.

Brinkley, Alan
1983 *Voices of Protest.* New York: Vintage.

Bruneau, Thomas
1986 "Brazil: The Catholic Church and Basic Christian Communities." In *Religion and Political Conflict in Latin America,* ed. Daniel H. Levine, 106–23. Chapel Hill: University of North Carolina Press.

Caretas (Lima)
1977 December 6.

CEAPAZ
1988 "Paz tarea de todos." Vol. 2 (January–March).

CELAM (Segunda Conferencia General del Episcopado Latino Smericano)
1968 "Los textos de Medellín." Vol. 1.

El Comercio (Lima)
1979a January 10.
1979b October 2.
1988 February 17.

Cordova, Daniel
1989 "El Programa de Asistencia Directa." In *Mujer y comedores populares,* ed. Nora Galer M. and Pilar Nuñez C., 65–72. Lima: SEPADE (Servicios para el Desarrollo).

Cotler, Julio
1987 *Clases, Estado y Nacion en el Peru.* Lima: Instituto de Estudios Peruanos.

Crespo Tarrero, Luis Fernando
1987 Interview with author, December 3.

Cuarderno (Lima)
1970 June 1.

Dammert Bellido, José
1988 Interview with author, May 3.

Degregori, Carlos Iván
1990 *El Surgimiento de Sendero Luminoso: Ayacucho 1969–1979.* Lima: Instituto de Estudios Peruanos.

DESCO Report
1989 *Violencia politica en el Perú: 1980–1988.* Vols. 1–2. Lima: DESCO, Centro de Extudios y Promocion del Dessarrollo.

Directorio
 1984 Eclesiastico del Perú. Lima.
 1987 Eclesiastico del Perú. Lima.

Durand Florez, Ricardo
 1991 Interview with author, June 24.

Durkheim, Emile
 1965 *The Elementary Forms of the Religious Life*. New York: Free Press.

Dussel, Enrique
 1981 *A History of the Church in Latin America: Colonialism to Liberation*. Grand Rapids, Mich.: Eerdmans.

Escrivá de Balaguer y Albás, Josemaría
 1939 *Camino*. Madrid: Scriptor, S.A.

Expreso (Lima)
 1974 May 9.

Exum, William H.
 1985 *Paradoxes of Protest*. Philadelphia: Temple University Press.

FE
 1986 *El desafío de la reconciliación* (proceedings of 1986 Conference on Reconciliation). Lima: APRODEA.

Ferree, Myra Marx, and Frederick D. Miller
 1985 "Mobilization and Meaning: Toward an Integration of Social, Psychological, and Resource Perspectives on Social Movements." *Sociological Inquiry* 55 (Winter): 38–61.

Figari, Luis Fernando
 1985 *Aportes para una teología de la reconciliación*. Lima: APRODEA.
 1988 Speech to the Encuentro de Espiritualidad, Centro Pastoral, Urbanización Monterrico, Lima. February 26.

Freeman, Jo
 1983 *Social Movements of the Sixties and Seventies*. New York: Longman.

Freire, Paulo
 1970 *Pedagogy of the Oppressed*. New York: Seabury.

Gamson, William A.
 1988 Political Discourse and Collective Action. In *From Structure To Action: Comparing Social Movement Research across*

Cultures, vol. 1, ed. Bert Klandermans, Hanspeter Kriesi, and Sidney Tarrow, 219–44. Greenwich, Conn.: JAI Press.

Gonzalez Umeres, Luz.
1988 Interview with author, January 28.

Gotay, Samuel Silva
1981 *El pensamiento christiano revolucionario en America Latina.* Salamanca: Ediciones Sígueme.

Gramsci, Antonio
1987 *Selections from the Prison Notebooks of Antonio Gramsci.* New York: International Publishers.

Gutiérrez, Gustavo
1973 *A Theology of Liberation.* New York: Orbis.
1984 *We Drink from Our Own Wells.* New York: Orbis.
1985 "Vaticano II y la Iglesia Latinoamericana." *Páginas* 70 (August): 2–12.
1988a Interview with author, April 15.
1988b "Path to Medellín." Lecture at annual summer workshop, Department of Theology, Pontifical Catholic University of Lima, February 10.

Hebblethwaite, Peter
1983 "Opus Dei: Lifting the Veil of Mystery." *National Catholic Reporter,* May 27.

Illich, Ivan
1967a "The Seamy Side of Charity." *America* 116 (January 21): 88–91.
1967b "The Vanishing Clergyman." *The Critic* 25 (June–July).

John Paul II
1982 "Opening Address at Puebla: Third General Conference of Latin American Bishops, Puebla de Los Angeles, Mexico, January 28, 1979." In *The Pope and Revolution: John Paul II Confronts Liberation Theology,* ed. Quentin L. Quade, 49–70. Washington, D.C.: Ethics and Public Policy Center.

Kamm, Henry
1984 "The Secret World of Opus Dei." *New York Times Magazine,* January 8.

Klaiber, Jeffrey
1983 "The Catholic Lay Movement in Peru." *The Americas* 40 (October): 149–70.

1988 *La Iglesia en el Perú.* Lima: Pontificia Universidad Catolica del Perú, Fondo Editorial.

Klandermans, Bert
1988 "The Formation and Mobilization of Consensus." In *From Structure to Action: Comparing Social Movement Research across Cultures,* vol. 1, ed. Bert Klandermans, Hanspeter Kriesi, and Sidney Tarrow. Greenwich, Conn.: JAI Press.

Kselman, Thomas A.
1986 "Ambivalence and Assumption in the Concept of Popular Religion," In *Religion and Political Conflict in Latin America,* ed. Daniel Levine, 24–41. Chapel Hill: University of North Carolina Press.

Kudó, Tokihiro
1982 *Hacia una cultura nacional popular.* Lima: DESCO.

Leo XIII
1891 "Rerum Novarum: The Condition of Labor." In *Catholic Social Thought: The Documentary Heritage,* ed. David J. O'Brien and Thomas A. Shannon, 12–39. New York: Orbis, 1992.

Lernoux, Penny
1982 *Cry of the People.* New York: Penguin.

Le Tourneau, Dominique
1986 *El Opus Dei.* Barcelona: Ediciones Oikos-Tau, S.A.

Levine, Daniel H.
1986 *Religion and Political Conflict in Latin America.* Chapel Hill: University of North Carolina Press.

Lizarzaburu, Pedro
1989 "Asistencia Alimentaria en el Peru." In *Mujer y comedores populares,* ed. Nora Galer M. and Pilar Nuñez C. 15–32. Lima: SEPADE.

McClintock, Cynthia
1989 "Peru's Sendero Luminoso Rebellion: Origins and Trajectory." In *Power and Popular Protest,* ed. Susan Eckstein, 61–101. Berkeley: University of California Press.

McGovern, Arthur F.
1990 *Liberation Theology and Its Critics: Toward an Assessment.* New York: Orbis.

McGuire, Meredith B.
1981 *Religion: The Social Context.* Belmont, Calif.: Wadsworth.

Maduro, Otto
1977 "New Marxist Approaches to the Relative Autonomy of Religion." *Sociological Analysis* 38 (Winter): 359–67.
1982 *Religion and Social Conflicts.* New York: Orbis.

Marka (Lima)
1975 November 13.

Marzal, Manuel
1983 *La transformacion religiosa peruana.* Lima: Pontificia Universidad Catolica del Peru.
986 *Historia de la antropologia indigenista: México y Perú.* Lima: Pontificia Universidad Catolica del Peru.

Matos Mar, José
1987 *Desborde popular y crisis del estado.* Lima: Instituto de Estudios Peruanos.

Merea, Emilio Valleguona
1985 "Prologo." In Luis Fernando Figari, *Aportes para una teología de la reconciliación,* 5–11. Lima: Fondo Editorial.

Montes, Ofelia
1987 "El comedor popular: De la gestión individual a la participación colectiva." In *Estrategias de vida en el sector urbano popular,* ed. Roelfien Haak and Javier Diaz Albertini, 75–94. Lima: FOVIDA-DESCO, Free Press.

Oberschall, Anthony
1973 *Social Conflicts and Social Movements.* Englewood Cliffs, N.J.: Prentice-Hall.

El Observador (Lima)
1982a March 28.
1982b April 3.
1983a January 27.
1983b February 3.

Orbegozzo y Goicoechea, Ignacio Maria de
1987a "Laicos en la Iglesia," *Revista Teologica Limense* 21 (May–August).
1987b "The Structure and Function of the Parish Council" (in Spanish). Document circulated by the Diocesan Office of Chiclayo to local parishes.

Paginás
1987 "Informe de Amnistia Internacional." *Paginás* 12 (March): 35.

Pásara, Luis
1986 *Radicalizacion y conflicto en la Iglesia peruana.* Lima: El Virrey.

Paul VI
1965 "Gaudium et Spes: Pastoral Constitution on the Church in the Modern World." In *Catholic Social Thought: The Documentary Heritage,* ed. David J. O'Brien and Thomas A. Shannon, 166–237. New York: Orbis Press, 1992.

Peña, Milagros
1994 "Liberation Theology in Peru: An Analysis of the Role of Intellectuals in Social Movements." *Journal for the Scientific Study of Religion* 33 (March): 34–45.

Piqueiras, Manuel
1991 Interview with author, June 18.

Pius XI
1931 "Quadragesimo Anno." In *Five Great Encyclicals,* 125–68. New York: Paulist Press, 1948.

Piven, Frances Fox, and Richard A. Cloward
1977 Poor People's Movements: Why They Succeed, How They Fail. New York: Pantheon.

La Prensa (Lima)
1978 April 9.
1979a September 25.
1979b September 28.

Ratzinger, Joseph
1984 "Instructions on Certain Aspects of the Theology of Liberation." *National Catholic Reporter,* September 21.

Realidad (Lima)
1979 May 3.

Rocca Salles, Ramon, ed.
1985 *Antología de textos.* Vol. 1 Chiclayo: ATENEO.

Romero, Catalina
1982 "Cambios en la relación iglesia-sociedad en el Perú: 1958–1978," *Debate* 7 (June): 115–41. Lima: Departamento de Ciencias Sociales (PUC).

1987 *Iglesia en el Perú: Compromiso y renovación (1958–1984).* Lima: Instituto Bartolomé de Las Casas.
1988 Interview with author, April 27.
1991 Follow-up interview with author, July.

Smith, Christian
1991 *The Emergence of Liberation Theology.* Chicago: University of Chicago Press.

Snow, David, and Robert D. Benford
1988 "Ideology, Frame Resonance, and Participant Mobilization." *International Social Movement Research* 1:197–217.

Snow, David, Burke E. Rochford Jr., Steven K. Worden, and Robert D. Benford
1986 "Frame Alignment Processes, Micromobilization, and Movement Participation." *American Sociological Review* 51:464–81.

Soriano, Waldermar Espinosa
1985 "La sociedad colonial y republicana (Siglos XVI a XIX)." In *Nueva historia general del peru: Un compendio,* 195–230. Lima: Mosca Azul Editores.

Stoll, David
1990 *Is Latin America Turning Protestant?* Berkeley: University of California Press.

Strong, Simon
1992 *Shining Path: The World's Deadliest Revolutionary Force.* New York: HarperCollins.

Tilly, Charles
1978 *From Mobilization to Revolution.* Reading, Mass.: Addison–Wesley.

Tovar, Teresa
1982 *Velasquismo y movimiento popular.* Ser. A, no. 4. Lima: DESCO.
1985 *Movimiento populares y crisis oligarquica (1900–1930).* Ser. B, no. 8. Lima: DESCO.
1986 "Movimiento Popular: Formacion y momento actual." In *Seminario realidad nacional,* pt. 2. Lima: Instituto Bartolomé de Las Casas.

Trapasso, Rosa Dominga
1988 Interview with author, April 19.

Ugarte, Ruben V.
1953 *Historia de la Iglesia en el Perú.* Vol. 1. Lima: Imprenta de Aldecoa.
1962 *Historia de la Iglesia en el Perú.* Vol. 5. Burgos: Imprenta de Aldecoa.

Vargas Ruíz de Somocurcio, Fernando
1988a Interview with author, March 24.
1988b "Liberación y Reconciliación en America Latina." Paper presented at the Bishops' Conference in Venezuela.

Vazquez De Prada, Andrés
1984 *El fundador del Opus Dei.* Madrid: Ediciones Rialp.

Vidales, Raúl
1993 Interview with author, August 1.

Villón, Jose Maguiña
1989 "Eficiencia de los comedores y nutrición." In *Mujer y comedores populares,* ed. Nora Galer M. and Pilar Nuñez C., 39–55.

Visión Peruana (Lima)
1986 November 2.

Weber, Max
1946 *Max Weber: Essays in Sociology.* Ed. H. H. Gerth and C. Wright Mills. New York: Oxford University Press.

Westhues, Kenneth
1973 "The Established Church as an Agent of Change." *Sociological Analysis* 34, no. 2: 106–23.

Whyte, John H.
1981 *Catholics in Western Democracies.* New York: St. Martin's.

INDEX